A PRACTICAL GUIDE
TO PROGRAM PLANNING
A Teaching Models Approach

A PRACTICAL GUIDE TO PROGRAM PLANNING

A Teaching Models Approach

ADRIANNE BANK

MARLENE HENERSON

LAUREL EU

Center for the Study of Evaluation
Graduate School of Education
University of California, Los Angeles

Teachers College, Columbia University
New York and London   1981

Published by Teachers College Press, 1234 Amsterdam Avenue, New York, N.Y. 10027

A Practical Guide to Program Planning: A Teaching Models Approach was developed under a contract with the National Institute of Education, Department of Health, Education and Welfare. However, the opinions expressed herein do not necessarily reflect the position or policy of that agency, and no official endorsement should be inferred.

Library of Congress Cataloging in Publication Data

Bank, Adrianne.
  A practical guide to program planning.

  Bibliography: p.
  Includes index.
  1. Elementary school teaching.   2. Curriculum planning.   I. Henerson, Marlene E.
II. Eu, Laurel.   III. Title.
LB1570.B325   372.11′02   81-959

ISBN 0-8077-2686-9 (cloth)
ISBN 0-8077-2641-9 (paper)   AACR2

Manufactured in the United States of America
86 85 84 83 82 81   1 2 3 4 5 6

Contents

Foreword

The word "teaching" suggests, more often than not, one person telling or showing others so that they will know or be able to do what they did not know or do previously. But there is much more to teaching than what shows "up front." Decisions must be made about what is to be learned and how best to structure the learning environment. Good teachers make many of the essential decisions long before teaching occurs. They depend heavily on their own background of education and personal experience as well as on knowledge of their students in planning their instructional program.

The authors of this book recognize the significance of this often lonely planning process and provide in this manual a comprehensive guide to each step. They address these steps in a way that provides teachers with a comprehensive understanding of planning, from first thoughts about the kinds of programs they desire to final thoughts about evaluating them. They include ideas for the experienced teacher as well as for the beginner, largely because they emphasize the need to think afresh. It is all too easy for a teacher to fall into routine ways of doing things, especially if he or she has taught the same grade or subject year after year.

The core of the book, however, is the detailed treatment of planning, organizing, teaching, and evaluating based on the assumptions and goals of five different models. Though each of these models grows out of alternative assumptions about learning, the models are not mutually exclusive. Rather, they represent the methods of conceptualization and implementation of several different kinds of learning in which people at various times engage. Students should have practice in these different modes; teachers should be able to construct learning situations likely to provide this practice. In effect, then, this part of the book is designed to assist teachers in developing the repertoire of planning, teaching, and evaluating skills inherent in each model.

The authors' approach is particularly timely. We are becoming increasingly aware of some of the abuses resulting from the excessive exhortation during the 1970's to get back to the basics. There is merit in the central idea that personal and vocational competence build from and on the ability to read, write, and compute. But there is no simple, mechanical formula for developing these basic skills or the complex reasoning ability for which reading, writing and computing are tools. Nonetheless, the search for and, indeed, use of some uniform pedagogical approach have been as intense during the past decade as at any time during our long, misguided search for panaceas. Analyses of standardized test scores are now beginning to show that students are deficient in the more complex learning processes such as concept learning and problem solving. We may be paying a price for too much emphasis on mechanistic practices of teaching and evaluating.

This emphasis, clearly apparent in state policy as well as practice, has tended, I believe, to push aside the significant results of inquiry into learning and, more recently, into teaching. Teachers are bombarded with how-to-do-it pedagogical procedures intended to prepare students to pass proficiency tests. What we need instead are translations of the accumulated wisdom of theorists and researchers into practical guidelines that will encourage creative thinking and planning by teachers. This text is an excellent example of such translation.

The authors have been highly selective. They have chosen five teaching models which, taken together, provide for a wide range of learning. They draw upon the investigations of just a few scholars in developing the assumptions of each model. Then they move quickly to the kind of learning embraced by each model, using practical examples. Next, the authors provide specific illustrations of how each model takes shape in the classroom. Again and again, they address the reader directly for purposes of assuring that she or he understands and is not merely memorizing each example. The assumption throughout is that teachers should *understand* the principles from which they can devise procedures appropriate to changing circumstances.

Not surprisingly, authors Adrianne Bank, Marlene Henerson, and

Laurel Eu stress the use of evaluation as a diagnostic tool in planning and teaching. Evaluation that measures only effects or outcomes ignores, for example, determination of the skills and understandings possessed by students at the beginning of a learning episode. With knowledge regarding students' entry behaviors at hand, teachers are in a better position to plan a range of activities appropriate to individual differences. With knowledge of how individual students are progressing, conscientious teachers redesign the instructional program in such a way as to provide for remediation or acceleration. Evaluation is a potentially powerful tool for program improvement.

All three authors have contributed to and internalized the philosophical position of the Center for the Study of Evaluation at UCLA's Graduate School of Education. From its beginning, the Center has stressed the use of evaluation for improving decisions in policy and practice. In keeping with the initial intent of educational laboratories and research and development centers created in 1965 through the Elementary and Secondary Education Act, the CSE has sought to link the academic community of theory and research with the community of educational practice. It has done this in part by developing materials for training administrators and teachers in planning and evaluating instructional programs.

This publication follows the spirit of previous contributions originating from the Center. Its purposes are to raise teachers' levels of awareness about the interdependence of planning, teaching, and evaluation and to provide teachers with practical help in carrying out these processes. Drawing as it does on knowledge about learning and the principles derived from this knowledge, it is an excellent sourcebook for everyday use.

JOHN I. GOODLAD
Professor and Dean
Graduate School of Education
University of California
Los Angeles, California

Acknowledgments

This book has gone through several incarnations since its inception in 1972 as a project of the Center for the Study of Evaluation, which was supported in turn by the National Institute of Education. We are grateful to the teachers, principals, evaluators, and other educators who stimulated each "rebirth."

We would like to thank in particular Dr. Marvin Alkin and Dr. Richard Seligman, who were Director and Associate Director of the Center during the early years of the project, for their encouragement and support, as well as Dr. Eva L. Baker, the current Director of CSE, for her help in carrying this book through to publication.

Past and present colleagues at CSE whose words and advice were much appreciated include Joyce DeMuth, Beverly Kooi, Tom Mann, Lynn Morris Mendelsohn, and Aleta Saloutos. A special thanks goes to Aurelia Arroyo and to Ruth Paysen for their tireless efforts on behalf of our manuscript. Finally, we particularly want to express our gratitude to Donna Cuvelier, who shepherded the book through its many lives with great competence and much good will.

PLANNING A
MODEL-BASED PROGRAM

1
Perspectives and Definitions

In many schools across the country teachers are looking for improved ways of helping children to learn. They may be supported in this effort by federal or state funds which provide them with the time and resources needed for systematic school-site program planning. But even without such extra funds, teachers—and often parents—may engage in planning efforts. This book is addressed to those individuals—teachers of students in kindergarten through eighth grade, administrators, parents—who would like to explore the use of teaching models as a basis for planning an educational program that has a good chance of upgrading student learning because of its built-in mechanisms for evaluation and improvement.

If you are a teacher in the public schools, you probably prepare a daily or weekly lesson plan. Most likely you also participate in more general activities that influence the direction of your school's educational program. Perhaps you have even served on committees to select textbooks, participated in in-service training to learn new classroom management techniques, or assisted in districtwide efforts to develop or revise a particular curriculum. However, though all of these efforts are related to planning educational programs, they do not encompass the totality of what we mean by program planning.

Program planning is a comprehensive endeavor which requires that philosophic and psychological assumptions, student activities, materials, and classroom organization be integrated with one another in such a way as to achieve a stated purpose and a set of explicit learning objectives. We believe that such events as the acquisition of texts, the development of teaching techniques, and the construction of curricular scope and sequence charts should not be considered in isolation from one another but rather as parts of a total educational effort.

One organizer you can use for developing an integrated program is called a teaching model. The five teaching models presented here did not originate with us; rather, they represent research-based psychological conceptualizations about how children learn. What we have done is to translate them into resources appropriate for classroom use. Each model includes classroom examples, step-by-step procedures, descriptions of classroom settings, expected student learning outcomes, and checklists for evaluating whether the essential features of the model have been implemented.

Planning a model-based program along with procedures to evaluate it rests on the assumption that you want to take a fresh look at what you are doing in your own classroom. This book provides the following resources to help you:

- tips and techniques for team planning
- a planning agenda for teaching and evaluating a model-based program
- descriptions of five teaching models representing a range of educational theories and applicable to a variety of subject areas. These include the concept analysis model, the creative thinking model, the experiential learning model, the group inquiry model, and the role-playing model.

The chapter on team planning will assist you in situations where a number of teachers come together to create a new course of study. It may be skipped, of course, if you are using this book by yourself.

The planning agenda presents a logical sequence for moving through planning and evaluation procedures. It includes a number of questions to help you explore the implications of each decision you will make.

The description of the five models will help you understand where each model came from and how its principles might translate into classroom practice. For each model there is also a list of references.

Before you read on, though, we want to define the terms we will be using.

Programs and their components

Educational programs come in many different sizes and shapes. The program you plan may be short or long—lasting several weeks, several months, or the whole school year. You may organize its presentation in a number of ways: for example, once a month, once a week, every day for an hour, or every day for all day. It may focus on a single subject area such as reading or science, or it may emphasize a process such as critical thinking or creativity and draw for its content on a number of subject areas. It may replace an existing program, or it may be a new addition. It may be intended for all the pupils in one or several grades, or for pupils with particular characteristics—for example, gifted children, bilingual children, or children with musical abilities.

But no matter how your program is organized, it should have one overriding characteristic: It should be a coherent and integrated set of learning activities supported by materials and teaching strategies in the service of a set of specific educational objectives.

Planning such a program means making decisions at a level of detail somewhere between day-to-day lesson planning and long-term curriculum planning. More specifically, model-based program planning calls for developing a structure within which your own teaching and your students' learning will occur. Such a structure includes:

- *philosophical or psychological assumptions:* your answers to questions like "What ought to be learned?" or "How does learning occur?"
- *objectives or anticipated outcomes:* the knowledge, skills, and attitudes that students will acquire as a result of their participation in the program
- *activities and procedures:* learning units in which students will engage, and the sequence in which these units will occur
- *setting:* the classroom organization within which activities will take place
- *materials:* software with which students will work—printed, visual, oral, or manipulative; commercially available or student-generated
- *evaluation:* the methods used for assessing the implementation and effectiveness of the program.

Teacher-generated programs and team planning

Educational programs originate from many sources. Publishers, for example, create programs in specific subject areas and then distribute them in the form of textbooks, workbooks, and teachers' guides. Often districtwide planning committees prepare curriculum guides and materials. Or, sometimes teacher teams plan programs for their own classes or grades, and either generate original materials or else use existing materials in fresh combinations. Advocates of this last approach believe it has the following advantages:

• *The resulting programs are more likely to fit the needs of the students than are commercially developed programs.* Teachers often complain that educational materials developed by publishers and chosen by administrators are inappropriate for their particular pupils. Though such materials can be modified or adapted, an individual teacher rarely has the time and resources for systematically carrying out such modification or adaptation. So revisions, if done at all, are made hurriedly in the teacher's spare time.

• *Such programs will fit the needs of teachers better.* In local planning, classroom teachers, not publishers, determine program priorities. In a team situation, teachers have the opportunity to share ideas and responsibilities, as well as to pool their professional expertise. A program planned by teachers is also likely to be more realistic than one planned externally; it will demand from teachers no more than they are able and willing to give.

• *Planning such programs can be professionally rewarding.* Planning is hard work and requires time. However, by setting aside some time for thinking about what is good for students, teachers increase their chances for professional growth and job satisfaction. Planning gives teachers the opportunity to reflect not only on what is good about their present practice but on what needs improvement.

Teaching, for some, is a lonely profession. In certain schools, teachers may have extensive contact with pupils but only minimal contact with colleagues. Sometimes teachers are unaware of what other teachers in the same school are doing; often they do not know that their colleagues have similar classroom problems and concerns. Such isolation can cause teachers to become discouraged and to feel as though their hard work is not appreciated.

In a planning team, however, teachers can share their experiences with one another and explore new ideas and materials. The experienced and successful teachers may need an antidote for the staleness of teaching the same grade or subject over and over again. As for the new teachers, they will profit from contact with their more experienced colleagues and be able to contribute fresh perspectives.

Teaching models

One major assumption underlying any teaching model is that *what* a child learns cannot be separated from *how* he or she learns. A teaching model is a method for integrating or making inseparable the *processes* of instruction and the *outcomes* of instruction, using a specific value system or learning theory as the unifying agent.

Bruce Joyce and Marsha Weil, who have done extensive work in developing materials and strategies for training teachers in the use of teaching models, note that

> a model of teaching is not a simple fixed formula for completing a job. It provides definite ideas for creating an environment from which students are likely to learn certain kinds of things, but it has to become a flexible, fluid instrument that is modified to fit different types of subject matter and that responds to students who are different from one another. . . . If one uses it too rigidly, it becomes a blunt instrument. If one holds it too lightly, it dissolves and becomes indistinguishable from any other method of teaching. It fails to do its work![1]

Although the five models provided in this guidebook differ from those described in the work of Joyce and Weil, it was their book, *Models of Teaching*,[2] which clarified the concept of a teaching model for us.

A second important assumption associated with the teaching model approach is that there is no single "correct" model for all classrooms or for all teachers. Most teachers, whether implicitly or explicitly, subscribe to a set of values and a theory of learning; consequently, their classroom practices conform, to a greater or lesser degree, to those values and to that theory. One teacher may believe that the primary purpose of education is to teach children conceptual skills; another may believe that the main goal is to help children get along with others; still another feels that children should develop confidence in themselves and a sense of personal worth. In short, teachers' classroom behaviors tend to reflect their own value positions, even if they have not articulated these positions to themselves or others.

In addition to holding value positions, teachers implicitly subscribe to theories about how children learn. Some believe that children learn primarily by doing and therefore organize their classrooms in a way that will maximize opportunities for pupils to touch, feel, and manipulate materials. Other teachers are more concerned with providing their students with consistent rewards for acceptable behavior, perhaps because they feel that reinforcement theories "work." Still others attempt to establish a classroom atmosphere that encourages children to try out new ideas without fear of failure.

A model-based approach to planning

A model-based approach to program planning requires the teacher to select a teaching model and to use it in developing a cohesive, logically consistent pattern of classroom activities. Still, a question you might ask is,

"If there are many valid teaching models, why not use an eclectic approach, selecting good ideas from various models of teaching?"

Although such an eclectic, or mixed, approach does characterize many educational programs, there are clear advantages to a model-oriented approach. If it is true that *what* children learn cannot be separated from *how* they learn, then consistency among the assumptions, objectives, and activities selected for use in the classroom, will ensure that the learning objectives are met. As teachers teach, they constantly make choices and establish priorities, even if they do not do so consciously. By planning, and using a model approach, they raise to the level of awareness the basis on which their choices are made in advance of their teaching.

When *you* start looking for a teaching model on which to base your own program, you will want to consider whether any of the models provided in this book comfortably fits your view of the world. Even if you are not certain of what that view is, the attempt to select an appropriate model may crystalize your thinking, since you must examine, in the process, the relationships among your philosophical assumptions, educational objectives, and classroom practices.[3]

Evaluation and program planning

You may wonder why, in a book oriented toward model-based planning, we have included a section on evaluation. While evaluation is often thought of as an activity that occurs after the completion of the program, this is not the way we define it. In our view, evaluation is the *systematic selection, collection, and interpretation of information that will be of use to you and to others who may make decisions about the program.*

Evaluative activities should inform your decisions at three major points: during the planning of the program, during the actual teaching of the program, and after the program has been completed and you are considering what to do next time.

When you develop a program using a teaching model approach, you will look to that model to provide the general structure for your program. Translating this general formulation into specific objectives will require that you have complete information about the current status of your pupils. Such data about the preprogram knowledge, skills, and attitudes of your students can help you define your program objectives.

You will also have to select appropriate activities to incorporate into the program. One question to ask yourself is the following: "Is the activity consistent with the main thrust of the model?" If you also ask yourself, "What evidence will I use to determine if the program is having the desired impact on my students?" your answer will help to establish a reliable connection between learning activities and anticipated student outcomes.

Evaluation and program revision

As you plan your program, you will be imagining new ways of instructing students, of organizing materials, and of arranging your classroom. Since these constitute only "best guesses" as to which classroom procedures are most likely to result in effective student learning, you may modify these plans as you go along. By documenting your own activities and those of the students—that is, by noting the way in which the program is actually implemented in the classroom—as well as by monitoring student learning at regular periods, you can judge which activities are working well and which ones should be revised or replaced.

After you have taught the entire program once, your cumulative evaluation data can help you to revise and improve it. The first time you teach a program there are likely to be various aspects you will want to change the next time around. Some of these you will identify intuitively; others you may come to identify only after you have data about the effect the total program had on your students. In either case, you will be able to make informed decisions about how to revise the sequence, pacing, activities, and materials of that program.

Evaluation and program replication

Evaluative information can help you justify your program to a funding agency or other teachers who might want to use it. If you want to obtain money to support the introduction of a new program in your school or to continue a program you feel has merit, you may have to submit to a funding agency your data or else a plan for obtaining information that will demonstrate and document its educational effectiveness. So it is important to consider such evaluative procedures early on.

Once you have taught the program, your evaluation of it will help others to understand your method. Such information can provide a thorough documentation of what you did and how the program affected your students, so that your colleagues will be able to decide whether the program is appropriate for their own students. In short, your own evaluation activities should start when you first think about the program, continue through the teaching of the program, and end only after final decisions have been made about recycling or disseminating the program to other teachers or to other schools.

2
Tips and Techniques for Team Planning

Whenever possible, the planning of a program should be carried out by teams comprised of interested teachers and parent representatives. This is especially desirable in the case of long-term or large-scale programs affecting several grades. It is less crucial if the program being contemplated is conducted within a single classroom under the control of a single teacher, or if there is little need to articulate the program with teachers in other grades.

Preconditions for team planning

Some benefits that can accrue from team planning of programs are:

- the creation of student-relevant programs
- the creation of teacher-feasible programs
- professional growth and development.

These benefits, however, come with costs attached to them, and willingness on the part of the school administration and the teachers to underwrite such costs is an essential precondition to embarking on a team planning effort. These costs include *time, money,* and *psychological support.*

Planning a program is time-consuming. Although dedicated teachers working many extra hours have been able to develop inventive programs without financial support, such "after-hours" procedures are not recommended. Better ways should be found—even though they might require additional funding—to make such team planning possible. These include providing release time for teachers (by hiring substitutes), paying for vacation or summer planning time, or hiring consultants to assist a program planning team.

Psychological support is almost as important as financial support for any program development effort. Key administrators in the district and in the school not only must value the program planning effort itself but must also support the idea of classroom innovation. The introduction of a new program into a school, even on a small scale, may be somewhat disruptive of normal operating procedures and may even create some strains for both participating and nonparticipating teachers. Therefore, the support of the administration and colleagues for the attempted changes is necessary to withstand early criticism made of the new proposals.

If a willingness to assume costs of program planning and development is one prerequisite for team planning, a second prerequisite is the creation of a reservoir of skills necessary to develop and implement such a program. These include:

- skills in group processes and decision making
- skills in program development and evaluation
- skills in subject matter
- skills in instructional management, especially those related to teaching models.

No one individual is likely to possess all of these skills. If some particular or critical skills are lacking, it may be possible (assuming the existence of financial resources) to hire consultants or trainers who have them.

A third prerequisite for team planning is attitudinal. This involves what might colloquially be described as a "spirit of adventure and daring." Individuals who begin to plan in groups usually are willing to break out of their old routines and take some risks. Still, they will need tough-mindedness to sustain themselves during the often frustrating and tedious processes of program creation and refinement. The excitement they feel because of these new possibilities and their dedication to "something better" may provide them with such sustenance.

Creating an effective planning team

Some of the features which enter into the creation of a good planning team are:

Number of team members. Although planning teams can range in size from two to a dozen people, the most effective team consists of three to six members. A team of this size ensures a working group even if someone is sick or temporarily overburdened. The group will be small enough, however, to require everyone's active participation and commitment to the planning effort.

Composition of team. People who have worked well together in the past and who know one another's styles form a good nucleus for any planning team. Individuals who share a concern for the pupils in the program, who have a thorough knowledge of the subject matter, or who have a special interest in instructional methods should also be included. In any event, the planning team should be composed of an ongoing group of teachers and parents, together with resource people who may be invited to individual meetings as needed.

Teachers. Planning-team members should include individuals who:

- will probably teach the program
- have the interest and knowledge needed to create the program
- share enough values so that communication among them is not difficult
- have "staying power" within a team situation (as demonstrated by their previous school responsibilities)
- have an intellectual predisposition toward planning—that is, an interest in talking about ideas and concepts that underlie what they teach
- are the opinion leaders of the school or have leadership qualities
- have schedules that allow them to meet at the appointed times.

Parents. Whether or not to include parents on the planning team is a decision that should be made by the team *after* the teacher members have been selected. (In some schools, and under some funding conditions, there may be a clearly established policy as to whether to include parents.)

Some advantages of having parents on the planning team are:

- They can introduce points of view not often heard by teachers.
- They will gain an increased understanding of the instructional process.
- They can create a sense of partnership in meeting the educational needs of the children.
- Their presence will help the school to comply with requirements for parent participation that exist in certain local, state, and federal programs.

Some disadvantages to including parents are:

- the potential difficulty of establishing communication between parents and teachers because of wide disparities in perspectives or knowledge
- the potential difficulty of finding parents who have the time and/or interest necessary for sustaining participation on a long-term basis
- the potential difficulty of selecting parents who will represent the normally wide range of parent concerns.

Among those who should be considered as parent members of a planning team are the following:

- parents who will probably have children in the program
- parents who are involved in major school-related organizations such as advisory councils, PTAs, etc.
- parents who have a specific expertise (i.e., former teachers, those having interest or experience in fields related to the various subject areas of the program, etc.).

Additional resource people. From time to time, the planning team may need to have consultants with particular skills attend one or more planning meetings. Consultants can include:

- those who have specific knowledge of instructional methods related to the teaching model
- those who have specific knowledge of instructional materials related to the teaching model
- those who have specific knowledge of the program's subject matter
- those who have specific skills in helping groups to communicate and to make decisions.

In short, a good planning team consists of individuals who can work well together, who are committed to what they are doing, and who have enthusiasm for and interest in the program being planned. As a team, they should possess a diversity of skills and perspectives, as well as have work schedules flexible enough to enable them to meet with one another whenever necessary.

Facilitating effective team processes

The suggestions listed below should help you hold effective meetings.

Leadership. A task-oriented group usually functions best with the guidance of a leader. Here are two possibilities for providing your group with appropriate leadership:

1. *Select one person as leader.* Having a single person as leader has the advantage of making clear exactly "who's in charge." As a result, the team members know who coordinates the team's work. A single leader can also maintain continuity from meeting to meeting, since he or she is aware of what has already happened and what should be done next. Finally, a single leader, with confidence in his leadership skills, will keep team members focused on the tasks to be accomplished.

2. *Rotate leaders, either automatically (i.e., in alphabetical or seating order) or voluntarily (i.e., having team members choose an assignment they feel particularly comfortable in handling).* This method, although lacking the clarity and continuity provided by the single leader method, has the advantage of dividing the responsibility for the preparation and conduct of the meetings and thus relieves any one individual of an overwhelming burden of work.

Whichever type of leadership your team chooses, however, it should be clear to all members well in advance of any meeting who is responsible for the conduct of that meeting.

Leadership requires that someone—usually the leader or else some other appointed individual—fulfill a number of crucial roles. These are:

- *summarizer*—to remind the group where it has come from, and where it is going, especially with reference to the announced agenda of the meeting
- *recorder*—to note who said what, what decisions were made, and what actions are to be taken
- *process facilitator*—to focus, when necessary, the group's attention on what is causing a breakdown in group functioning.

Communication. Good communication within a small group demands that each individual be both a clear sender and an accurate receiver of messages. This communication is different from the one-way communication that occurs in a lecture, where a single person (the speaker) sends a message to many people (the audience).

Considerable skills are needed in sending and receiving messages. Awareness and practice of these skills will help group members eliminate some of the "static" which can interfere with effective communication.

To *send* clear messages, team members should:

- describe a situation as factually as possible
- express their feelings in a way that clearly shows they own the feelings—e.g., "I feel upset because this meeting isn't accomplishing anything," rather than "Everyone here is talking too much."
- introduce their conclusions or opinions with a phrase which clearly

identifies them as such—e.g., "I think that we should protest that situation," rather than "The only thing to do is to file a protest."

To make sure a message has been clearly *received*, team members should:

• paraphrase the substance of what the other person has said and make sure that the paraphrase is acceptable

• check perceptions—e.g., describe one's understanding of the other person's feelings without any interpretations, analyses, or expressions of approval or disapproval, and then check to see that this description is acceptable.

Developing the foregoing skills will help clarify discussion by distinguishing the "I don't understand what you mean" statements from the "I don't agree with what you are saying" statements.

Decision making. Groups sometimes get bogged down in controversies which seem to have no resolution. To deal with this, the leader might:

• *summarize areas of agreement* by asking individuals to list what they feel the group agrees to and then to review each entry and modify it until a consensus is reached

• *redefine the areas of disagreement* by asking participants to summarize their own positions and the position with which they disagree and then to suggest modifications that would make the position acceptable to them

• *get participants to negotiate or compromise* by asking them to make trade-offs—e.g., to agree to someone else's position in exchange for getting their own opinion accepted in some other area

• *seek new information or new perspectives* by requesting that an outside observer be brought in to offer either new information or a new perspective, thus making it easier to reach a decision

• *postpone a decision,* since it is often better to leave the decision pending than to reach a hasty or unsatisfactory conclusion. Work can then be done in the interim on clarifying the problem so that progress can be made at the next meeting.

Idea generation. Everyone should be encouraged to contribute ideas and to make suggestions. Two possible methods for achieving this are:

1. *Brainstorming.* Individuals, after agreeing on the statement of a problem, suggest possible solutions in a rapid "stream-of-consciousness" fashion. A recorder lists them on a blackboard or a large sheet of paper. The notion underlying brainstorming is that one person's ideas will stimulate additional ideas in other people. One important rule to remember is *not* to allow criticism or evaluation. No one should say, "That

won't work," "That's not relevant," "We tried that before," "That's silly." Instead, after the first phase of the brainstorming session has ended, ideas should be combined, classified, examined for their usefulness, and then accepted or discarded.

2. *Individual generation of ideas followed by group discussion.* Individuals should work by themselves or else in pairs for a prescribed period of time on an agreed-upon problem. Someone should keep notes on their ideas and conclusions and then present these to the group. It is often helpful if these notes (or summaries) are written in a way that everyone can readily see them. Once this is done, ideas may be combined, classified, examined for their usefulness, and then accepted or discarded.

Checklist for team leaders

Preparation for the meeting

☐ 1. Acquaint yourself with the tasks the group will try to accomplish (see the step-by-step procedures in Chapter 3).

☐ 2. State, in your own words, the tasks the team will be attempting to accomplish at the meeting.

☐ 3. Estimate the amount of time the team will need to accomplish each task.

☐ 4. As you review the tasks, identify those which can be completed in advance of the meeting and those which someone should prepare for general discussion.

☐ 5. Try to anticipate topics which are likely to engender argument or disagreement.

☐ 6. Rehearse in your mind what you will do in the event that problems of group interaction occur.

☐ 7. Make up an agenda that allocates time for tasks and for breaks.

☐ 8. Double-check details such as availability of the meeting room, refreshments, materials, adequate seating, blackboards, chalk, etc.

☐ 9. Send to all team members a note reminding them of the date, time, and place of the meeting; if possible, include the agenda.

Conduct of the meeting

☐ 1. Establish a comfortable atmosphere so that everyone feels free to express an opinion on whatever subject is under discussion.

☐ 2. Make sure the members don't wander off the subject or go off on tangents.

☐ 3. Be aware that some people may be more reluctant to volunteer ideas than others, and that some may want to bring up unrelated matters. (In this regard, remember that everyone will soon feel a sense of frustration if the meeting is not accomplishing anything or if some members are not contributing.)

☐ 4. Ask someone to act as recorder of the meeting and to take notes. (It is very important to have an accurate record of all decisions made by the team.)

☐ 5. Have team members introduce themselves, if they are not already known to one another.

☐ 6. Make sure everyone understands what you will be trying to accomplish at the meeting. (Review the agenda and ask for modifications or suggestions.)

☐ 7. Keep track of the time so that your agenda is completed by the end of the meeting. (You might wish to appoint someone to watch the clock and keep the group on schedule.)

☐ 8. Summarize the discussion at various points during the meeting, or appoint someone else to do this.

☐ 9. Encourage everyone to speak, either by going around the table asking for opinions, or by calling directly on those who have not yet offered an opinion.

☐ 10. At the end of the meeting, discuss briefly what participants liked and did not like about the meeting.

☐ 11. Recapitulate the decisions that were made and acknowledge those that were not agreed upon. (Make sure the recorder has included all this information in the minutes of the meeting.)

☐ 12. Plan how to improve future meetings.

☐ 13. Schedule the time and place for the next meeting and discuss the tasks to be accomplished then.

3
A Planning Agenda

The planning agenda that we will be discussing in this chapter involves four basic steps. Each step in turn is broken down into a number of subheadings. Although the steps are sequenced chronologically, you should keep all of them in mind as you consider and then complete each step. For example, you should be aware, before starting Step 1, that some of the evaluation procedures outlined in Step 4 are supposed to occur concurrently with the activities listed in Steps 1 and 3.

The four steps are:

STEP 1: Program Formulation
STEP 2: Model Selection
STEP 3: Program Planning
STEP 4: Program Evaluation

In *Step 1*, you will think about what you hope to accomplish in your new program. As you begin to describe it, make some tentative decisions about what areas you wish to emphasize and which skills you expect your students to develop. You should also think about your own capabilities, your roles and responsibilities as a teacher, and the potentialities and constraints in your classroom and school situation. *In Step 1, you will develop a description of the kind of program you want for your students, including such administrative specifics as number of students, number of teachers, length of program, subject matter, etc.*

In *Step 2*, you will select one or more of the five teaching models summarized on pages 30–35 that are compatible with your point of view about learning, and that seem to be suited to your pupils and to your unique teaching situation. You will want to compare these models with one another as well as with your own program ideas. To learn more about a prospective model, you can either do some further reading or else locate classrooms where you can observe part or all of a model in operation. You may even decide to experiment with some part of a model-based procedure in your own classroom before you make your final selection. *In short, by the end of Step 2 you will have tentatively selected one or more models on which to base your program.*

In *Step 3*, you will use this selection when deciding upon the objectives, student activities, materials, and sequences for your program. This step, you will find, is the most demanding of all. Therefore, you may want to factor into your program planning additional information about the students derived from the assessment activities described in Step 4.

If you are seeking funds for your program, you might want to prepare a written document outlining your program plans in detail. If you have no need for such a document, however, you may prefer to produce a set of notes which you can refer to later when you teach your program. In either case, you will need to have something on paper, particularly if more than one person is involved in planning, implementing, and evaluating the program. The amount of detail and degree of formality you want in your written plan will depend on your individual situation and on who, besides yourself, will need to know about the program. *In short, by the end of Step 3 you will have created either a formal or an informal program plan.*

Step 4 will help you to think about the evaluation of your program. After you have finished Step 3 (but before you begin to teach your program) take the time to build in procedures for describing what is happening in your classroom and for ascertaining what types of student learning are occurring. You should also identify the time periods when you will review these data so that you can make within-course corrections. Simultaneously, you will be keeping a record of this process and progress data that will enable you to take an end-of-the-program look at your total effort so that you can make informed judgments about what to do next. *All these steps will ensure that, by the end of Step 4, you will have an evaluation plan cross-referenced to your program plan so that you can determine how your program might be improved. At the same time, you will have collected sufficient information about the program to justify your application for dissemination funds.*

NOTE: If you are working in a planning team, you may want to determine the approximate number of meetings that will be required to work through the procedures for each step. A tentative schedule can be devised by someone on the team who has the time to review *all four steps* prior to the first meeting of the group. Figure 1 (beginning on page 20) outlines in considerable detail the four steps and tasks in the planning agenda. Also provided are checks and dates that indicate how one particular planning team scheduled its assignments and meetings over a one-year period.

Step 1: Program Formulation

Overview of Step 1

   A. Think about the intended emphases of your program.
   B. Identify your own roles and responsibilities as a teacher as you see them.
   C. Think about the students who will participate in the program and gather information about them if necessary.
   D. Consider what is possible and practical.

A. Think about the intended emphases of your program.

Your own professional growth and renewal and the building of networks of communication with your colleagues and peers are two very real and important reasons to devote time and energy to planning a new program. But, important as they are, they are not the ultimate purpose for such a program. Above everything else, you are planning a program for students, and it is *their skills, achievements, and growth that will be the measure of your program's success.*

We all have a tendency, when we think of instruction, to focus on what we ourselves will do. We say: "We will cover . . ." or "We will use . . ." or "We'll develop a program to teach our kids how to. . . ." However, we urge you to move beyond this approach as you consider what your program should emphasize. In putting your thoughts into writing, make sure they also include phrases or statements about what the *students* will learn or achieve in your program. Notice how the following examples contain clear statements about intended *student* outcomes:

   • "We need a program to provide remedial work for eighth graders so that by the end of the year *they will have the appropriate basic math skills.*"

   • "Our program will help *students to learn to respect and get along with people of different backgrounds.*"

   • "In our program we will prepare *students with limited skills in understanding English to move into classrooms where instruction is provided in English.*"

   • "We want this program to give *students an introduction to literature so that they will come to enjoy reading poetry, essays, plays, and novels.* We would also like *our students to begin to discriminate between good writing and poor writing."*

• "This program is going to introduce children to formal schooling. Its purpose, therefore, will be *to teach them how to function effectively in a school setting and to help them develop positive attitudes toward school."*

• We want a program to help our *children develop logical thinking skills that will serve as the foundation for future learning."*

All these statements of program intention are *student*-oriented, though obviously they vary in terms of their educational emphases. The first statement stresses *subject matter knowledge* (e.g., basic math); another, *social interaction skills* (e.g., respect for others and the ability to get along with them); and still another, the acquisition of *information processing skills* (e.g., developing the ability to think logically).

Just as the models in this manual emphasize one or another of these various kinds of learning, so your program will stress one or more of these approaches. Of course, you need not make a final decision now; in fact, you may change your mind several times while reading the model descriptions. You do need a place to start, though. So, before you move on to consider the models themselves, think about the following question:

Do we most want our students to . . .

• acquire subject matter knowledge?
• develop information processing skills?
• develop social interaction skills?

B. Identify your own roles and responsibilities as a teacher as you see them.

It is quite likely that five different teachers could begin with the same statement about program emphasis and yet each would develop a different type of program. Such diversity is understandable; but, if planning or teaching is to occur as a team, the ultimate statement should not mask real differences among the team members, nor should fellow teachers work in a program which they don't understand or with which they disagree. Either collectively or individually, you should design an educational program with an emphasis that makes sense to you, that takes advantage of your individual and unique talents, and that reflects a point of view on learning with which you fully agree. In so doing, you must take the time to identify your own strengths (and weaknesses) and to become aware of your assumptions about how children learn. Methods for achieving this kind of introspection or analysis can range from elabo-

(Continued on page 24)

Figure 1. Four Steps in a Planning Agenda

Tasks to Be Accomplished	Individually	As a Team	Date of Meeting
STEP 1. Program Formulation			
A. Think about the intended emphases of your program.			
A1. Read part A.	✓		
A2. Generate list of possible program emphases.		✓	9/30
A3. Make sure that list includes what students will learn or do.		✓	9/30
A4. Make a tentative selection of two or three emphases.		✓	10/7
B. Identify your own roles and responsibilities as a teacher as you see them.			
B1. Read part B.	✓		
B2. Discuss your strengths, preferences, opinions.			
B3. Compare yours with those of other planning team members.		✓	10/14
C. Think about the students who will participate in the program and gather information about them if necessary (see Step 4A).			
C1. Read part C.	✓		
C2. Read Step 4A.	✓		10/14
C3. Discuss entry characteristics of prospective students.		✓	
C4. Decide if you require additional information for planning your program evaluation.		✓	10/21
D. Consider what is possible and practical.			
D1. Read part D.	✓		10/27
D2. Make tentative decisions about total amount of instructional time needed (how many hours a week for how many weeks); number of students served; budget that is available; facilities and equipment needed.		✓	11/4

Figure 1 (continued)

Tasks to Be Accomplished	Individ-ually	As a Team	Date of Meeting
STEP 2. Model Selection			
A. Read the summaries of the five teaching models, compare them, and select one or two that seem suitable to you.			
A1. Read part A.	✓		
A2. Discuss summaries and make an initial selection.		✓	11/18
B. Read the extended descriptions of the five models.			

B1. For each model, discuss:
       assumptions
       pupil outcomes
       activities
       program organization.
		✓	12/2

C. Become more informed about each of your likely models.			

C1. Assign to one or more people the responsibility for further exploration of models, such as:
       literature search
       locating programs which use the models
       classroom tryouts.
		✓	12/2

C2. Discuss results of exploratory activities and assign observation or tryout responsibilities.		✓	12/16
C3. Discuss information obtained from observations or tryouts.		✓	1/16
C4. Make final selection of model(s).		✓	1/16

(Continued)

Figure 1 (continued)

Tasks to Be Accomplished	Individually	As a Team	Date of Meeting
STEP 3. Program Planning			
A. Decide on the outcomes you expect students in your program to achieve.			
A1. Read relevant sections of the chosen model.	✓		
A2. Extract and write down possible program objectives from the model.		✓	1/13
A3. Rewrite these to conform to your own subject matter or learning episodes.	✓		
A4. Brainstorm about related behaviors for each program objective.		✓	1/22
A5. Critique and refine program and institutional objectives.		✓	1/29–2/10
B. Decide on the essential characteristics of the learning activities.			
B1. Review model checklists.	✓		
B2. Discuss how to distinguish model-related from nonmodel-related actions.		✓	2/26
B3. Write up one prototype activity.		✓	
B4. Develop sets of activities.	✓		3/4
C. Decide on program organization.			
C1. Schedule a time line for activities.	✓	✓	3/11
D. Finalize your program plan.			
D1. Write your program plan.	✓	✓	3/19

Figure 1 (continued)

Tasks to Be Accomplished	Individ-ually	As a Team	Date of Meeting
STEP 4. Program Evaluation			
A. Decide on the evaluation questions you want to answer (1) for the program planning phase; (2) for the program revision phase; (3) for the program replication phase.			
A1. Recall your description of students likely to be in program (minutes from 10/21) and decide on data collection related to preprogram skills of students.		✓	4/10
A2. Discuss evaluation questions related to program revision and select several.		✓	4/17
B. Decide on procedures for answering each evaluation question.			
B1. Decide to use consultant or else decide yourselves on these procedures.		✓	4/24
C. Develop an evaluation plan that is coordinated with your program plan.			
C1. Draw up evaluation management plan and construct time line.		✓	5/6

rate (e.g., use of a tool like the Minnesota Teacher Attitude Inventory[1]) to simple (e.g., jotting down your thoughts about your own educational viewpoint as well as your strengths and weaknesses in the classroom). However you do it, asking yourself the following questions can help to channel your thinking:

1. What are my strengths as a teacher?
   - Am I most effective in helping students learn subject matter information? Work well with one another? Develop logical thinking skills? Feel good about themselves and their accomplishments?
   - How effective am I in working with pupils individually? In small groups? In large groups?
   - Are there certain kinds of students with whom I work particularly well? With whom I feel less comfortable?
   - In what ways would I like to improve or grow as a teacher?
2. What kind of classroom atmosphere do I prefer?
   - How much noise and movement will I tolerate?
   - Can I work comfortably when colleagues or other adults are in the classroom?
   - What kinds of seating arrangements for students have I already used? Would I like to introduce?
   - How willing am I to experiment with new kinds of classroom settings? New kinds of teaching materials?
3. What do I think are the classroom conditions which help children to learn? Prevent them from learning?
   - What activities do I myself find productive?
   - What decisions about what to learn and when to learn it am I willing to leave in the hands of students?
   - How much content do I myself usually provide to the students? To what degree am I willing to let them teach one another? How much do I expect them to get on their own from individual study?
   - Am I ready to try new techniques? Teach in a different style, if necessary?

C. Think about the students who will participate in the program and gather information about them if necessary.

If you are developing an instructional program for students who you believe are similar to those you are now teaching, you may already know what they can do and cannot do. For example, you may anticipate difficulty in getting them to engage in such activities as role playing or small group inquiry. You may already know that your students tend to have difficulties with particular subject areas. In fact, it could be that these very problems with subject matter are influencing you to seek alternative and better approaches. Or perhaps you have begun to feel strongly that unless your students learn more about interpersonal skills and appropriate classroom behaviors, it matters little what subject matter you attempt to teach to them.

We have provided suggestions for more formal preprogram assessment activities in Step 4. You may want to use some of them, or else you may simply want to take note of whatever informal information or data are already available to you. Think, too, about what the students are like in terms of

• *their abilities and attitudes:*   At what level of achievement will they be coming into the program? With what strengths? What weaknesses? How wide is their range of abilities?

• *their previous instruction:*   Have some students received more classroom and/or home exposure than others in terms of concepts to be learned? Do certain teaching strategies work better than others for particular pupils?

• *group characteristics:*   Are there large numbers of students whose English-speaking ability is limited? What percentage are gifted students? Students with learning disabilities? Is there great economic or cultural diversity reflected in the group? In what way may these characteristics affect your decisions?

• *future considerations:*   Will students be tested in the near future and, if so, in what areas? What skills, attitudes, or subject matter knowledge will they be expected to have in order to perform successfully the work at the next grade level?

D. Consider what is possible and practical.

Your program—in fact, any program—will have to function with certain constraints of time, equipment, materials, and budget. Take these constraints into account at the beginning of your planning effort. A short, modest program in which students achieve a limited set of objectives will be much more useful in the long run than an overly ambitious program which leaves everyone feeling dissatisfied because of the discrepancy between what was hoped for and what was actually achieved. If you start out small and are successful, you can use that success to justify a more ambitious undertaking later.

But what is possible and practical? In considering this basic question, ask yourself the following:

- How many instructional hours are available for teaching the new program? Divided over how many weeks, months, etc.?
- How much money is available? Enough to purchase materials, equipment? To hire aides?
- What facilities are available? Is there access to the library? The auditorium? Resource rooms?
- Can the program count on the assistance of parents? Aides? Counselors? Consultants?
- How much flexibility is there in arranging the furniture in the classroom? Scheduling field trips? Developing instructional schedules?

After you answer these questions, you may want to summarize for yourself the preliminary decisions you have made about the kind of program you want for your students in terms of the following six categories:

- Program emphasis
- Number of students to be served
- Types of students and their needs
- Number of instructional hours available: _____ (_____ hours per week for _____ weeks)
- Available budget: start-up $_____; ongoing $_____.
- Necessary facilities, equipment, etc.

NOTE: If you are working in a planning team, the preceding questions can serve as the basis for discussing each member's beliefs, strengths, and weaknesses. This in turn may lead to the decision to team-teach so that different teachers share responsibility for portions of the program. Or, you may find that, as a team, you would like to improve your collective skills in a particular instructional method or try something you have never done before. However, wait to confront the issue of how to improve your skills until *after* you have finished planning and have a total picture of what your program will be.

Step 2: Model Selection

Overview of Step 2

A. Read the summaries of the five teaching models, compare them, and select one or two that seem most suitable to you.
B. Read the extended descriptions of the five models.
C. Become more informed about each of your likely models.

A. Read the summaries of the five teaching models, compare them, and select one or two that seem most suitable to you.

On the next few pages you will find summaries of each of the five teaching models discussed in this book. As you read them, notice that each includes whatever assumptions are implicit in a particular model, the type of teacher behavior called for in using each model, the student outcomes likely to result from model-based instruction, the suitability of each model for particular grades and subject areas, and finally, the considerations and precautions that should be kept in mind when introducing a model-based program.

Try also to answer these questions after considering each summary:

- Does this model express a point of view about learning with which I agree?
- Is this model suitable for the kind of program I have in mind?
- Does the model call for teacher behavior with which I would be comfortable?
- Does it call for activities appropriate for the pupils?
- Can I achieve the classroom organization and obtain the materials called for in this model?
- Can I handle problems which might arise by using this model?

After you've answered the above questions, you should be ready to select the model that seems most suitable for your program. If there is *more* than one model that appeals to you, you may prefer to use some of the points of view and activities of two different models and combine them in some compatible form. For example, you may decide to use role-playing activities within the structure of the creative thinking model. Or, you might select the group inquiry model to provide the overall structure for your program and the creative thinking model to provide the techniques for guiding the inquiry. In any event, it is best to postpone the final selection of a model until *after* you've completely worked your way through Step 2.

NOTE: If you are working in a planning team, the preceding questions can serve as the basis for discussing and comparing the five model summaries. (These questions are restated in chart form in Figure 2 and Figure 3; they can be completed if the team is having difficulty reaching consensus.)

The first chart (Figure 2) should be filled in by individual team members. The second (Figure 3) should then be completed by the person serving as the team secretary, who will base his or her entries on the responses of all team members. By tabulating these responses, the team can easily compare the scores achieved by each model in each of the six categories included in Figures 2 and 3.

(Continued on page 30)

Figure 2. Individual Chart for Comparing Teaching Models

	Concept Analysis	Creative Thinking	Experiential Learning	Group Inquiry	Role Playing
1. Does this model express a point of view about learning with which I agree?					
2. Is this model suitable for the kind of program I have in mind?					
3. Does the model call for teacher behavior with which I would be comfortable?					
4. Does it call for activities appropriate for the pupils?					
5. Can I achieve the classroom organization and obtain the materials called for in this model?					
6. Can I handle problems which might arise by using this model?					

NOTE: 3 = yes; 2 = undecided; 1 = no.

Figure 3. Team Chart for Comparing Teaching Models

	Concept Analysis				Creative Thinking				Experiential Learning				Group Inquiry				Role Playing			
	Team Member				Team Member				Team Member				Team Member				Team Member			
	1	2	3	4	1	2	3	4	1	2	3	4	1	2	3	4	1	2	3	4
1. Does this model express a point of view about learning with which we agree?																				
2. Is this model suitable for the kind of program we have in mind?																				
3. Does the model call for teacher behavior with which we would be comfortable?																				
4. Does it call for activities appropriate for our pupils?																				
5. Can we achieve the classroom organization and obtain the materials called for in this model?																				
6. Can we handle problems which might arise by using this model?																				
TOTALS: Individual																				
Overall																				

NOTE: 3 = yes; 2 = undecided; 1 = no.

Model summaries

1. CONCEPT ANALYSIS MODEL[2]

This model provides pupils with systematic instruction on how to process subject-related information. It is based on the assumption that pupils should be taught all the basic concepts in a subject area, and that they should be given directed practice in classification and discrimination skills. With this type of instruction, they will learn sets of subject-related concepts that will provide them with a solid foundation for further learning.

To use this model successfully, teachers must be able to

- select important subject-related concepts that are at an appropriate level for their pupils
- analyze the concepts in order to determine the difficulty they will pose for their pupils
- monitor pupils' understanding of each concept
- schedule instruction according to accepted principles of learning and developmental theory.

If this model is used properly, pupils should improve their ability to

- recognize phenomena which do or do not exhibit described features or attributes
- identify features or attributes of their environment that belong together or relate to one another
- discover and then use categories (concepts) which will enable them to make sense of their environment.

Suitability. This model stresses subject matter content and information processing. It is most appropriate for social studies, math, and science, but can be used with most areas of the curriculum. The model may also be used with children at kindergarten through eighth-grade level.

Considerations and precautions. This model will require teachers to devote much time to preparing materials and sequencing their instruction. Teachers must first isolate and then analyze each concept they wish to teach and, if necessary, improve their own understanding of these concepts. They should likewise determine the extent to which each pupil comprehends the concept(s) being studied.

Whenever possible, materials used with this model should be made manipulable, and the instructional activities be made interesting and enjoyable to the pupils. Materials as well as activities must accommodate several levels of conceptual difficulty in order to be challenging to students. Appropriate assessment procedures and instruments should be developed to ascertain the status of individual pupils.

Generally speaking, well-organized teachers who have subject area specialties will find they are comfortable with this particular model.

2. CREATIVE THINKING MODEL[3]

This model is designed to increase the fluency, flexibility, and originality with which pupils approach objects, events, concepts, and feelings. It is based on the assumption that pupils can and should be taught techniques that will stimulate their creativity. The classroom atmosphere should be one in which divergent responses are respected and rewarded. Pupils who learn a repertoire of creative techniques can use them to deal more effectively with problems encountered in any given subject area.

To use this model successfully, teachers must be able to

- establish an atmosphere in which all ideas are welcome, not only for their immediate usefulness but also for their originality and their potential to lead to new ideas and directions
- help pupils become aware of inadequacies and discrepancies in commonly held explanations and beliefs
- help pupils become more open and sensitive to their environment
- insure the absence of a formal, "testlike" atmosphere which can only inhibit student creativity and original thinking
- provide stimuli that will afford practice in clear thinking.

If the model is used appropriately, pupils will learn to

- develop attitudes conducive to creative thinking
- use problem reformulation techniques to generate new ideas
- recognize discrepancies in ideas and use this awareness to generate new ideas
- employ analogies as a way to generate new ideas.

Suitability. This model emphasizes information processing and personal growth skills. It is most appropriate for science, social studies, and language arts, but is also applicable to other areas of the curriculum. It is most suitable for children in grades 3 through 8.

Considerations and precautions. Specific materials or situations must be found or developed which will stimulate creative thinking. They should contain oddities, puzzlements, obvious discrepancies, or mysteries which will lead to multiple or unusual responses. Of paramount importance is the teacher's willingness to find merit in a variety of responses, to dispel the notion that there is a single correct answer, and to allow pupils sufficient time to think and mull over their ideas.

Teachers who are not overly concerned about grades, who themselves enjoy "playing with" ideas, and who are willing to allow a class activity or discussion to veer off in unplanned directions are most likely to be comfortable with this particular model.

3. EXPERIENTIAL LEARNING MODEL[4]

This model provides pupils with opportunities to act upon their environment in such a way as to acquire thinking skills not related to any specific subject area. It is based on Piaget's findings that cognitive development occurs when children interact with ambiguous or seemingly contradictory aspects of their environment. If this model is used, therefore, class time should be filled with activities that pique children's curiosity and are absorbing to them. Young children, in particular, need time to "play with" and "do things to" concrete objects and materials in order to see for themselves "what happens."

To use this model successfully, teachers must be able to

- provide a wide variety of concrete materials for pupils to manipulate and examine
- allow pupils a sufficient range of activities to assure their interest and involvement
- arrange activities in such a way that pupils at different stages of cognitive development will learn from one another
- develop questioning techniques to elicit from students the reasons underlying their responses
- create a classroom environment that will promote the development of cognitive processes.

If this model is used appropriately, pupils will tend to

- develop problem-solving skills, particularly those involving number, measurement, and space
- increase their awareness of the regularity and predictability of the natural environment
- develop peer relationships that will help promote social and cognitive development
- assume responsibility for their own actions.

Suitability. Deriving as it does from Piaget's work, this model emphasizes the ways in which information processing, personal growth, and social interaction skills are acquired by children. It is especially applicable to math, science, and language arts, but it can be used in other areas of the curriculum as well. It is particularly appropriate for children in kindergarten through third grades, though it can also be used with children in the upper elementary grades.

Considerations and precautions. This experiential learning model calls for flexibility in classroom arrangements and requires that pupils have latitude in selecting their own daily activities. The materials they use must be discovery oriented rather than drill oriented. Adult help in preparing and maintaining the materials as well as in assisting and observing the pupils as they work is very useful.

Teachers introducing this model should develop a system that will help them keep track of each child's progress even when everyone is doing something different. A class in which there is much individual activity can easily become chaotic unless the teacher has the skill and willingness to monitor and guide the students in this kind of setting.

4. GROUP INQUIRY MODEL[5]

This model teaches children to work in groups as they investigate complex topics. The model assumes that the ability to pursue and complete tasks within a group setting is essential in both classroom and nonclassroom situations. Children who can participate in such group problem-solving activities will have the social skills necessary for approaching a variety of subjects in a productive way.

To use this model effectively, teachers must be able to

- help pupils define interesting or puzzling situations that are amenable to research
- teach pupils basic research and evaluative skills needed for successful inquiry
- help pupils learn skills that are necessary for successful group work
- allow pupils to conduct their own groups and make their own decisions.

If this model is used appropriately, pupils will learn to

- develop the ability and willingness to articulate their own viewpoints within a group setting
- identify questions amenable to research and seek answers to these questions
- plan their research
- participate effectively in group decision making
- take responsibility for completing their assigned tasks
- present and evaluate what they have discovered in the course of their research.

Suitability. Since this model emphasizes task-oriented social interaction skills, it is most appropriate for science and social studies programs and for children in grades 4 through 8.

Considerations and precautions. The group inquiry model requires teachers to achieve a balance between providing pupils with instruction in crucial skills and allowing them to proceed independently and to learn from their own mistakes. It also demands that many resources be accessible to the pupils to enable them to carry out their research—if not in the classroom, then in local libraries or museums, or the community. If the class is large, adult assistants can help answer pupils' questions and move along group activities. Teachers who use this model must take care that they guide, *not* mandate, the decisions made by the children.

5. ROLE-PLAYING MODEL[6]

This model provides pupils with practice in putting themselves into roles and situations that will increase their awareness of their own and other people's values and beliefs. Role playing can help them understand why they and other people think and act as they do. In the process of "trying on" roles of people who are different from themselves, pupils can learn about both the diversity and similarity of human behavior and can apply this learning in real-life situations.

To use this model successfully, teachers must be able to

- present, or help pupils select, appropriate role-playing situations
- establish a supportive atmosphere that encourages pupils to act "as if" without embarrassment
- manage the role-playing situations in such a way as to encourage spontaneity and learning
- teach observation and listening skills so that students can observe and listen to one another effectively and then interpret accurately what they see and hear.

If this model is used appropriately, pupils will learn to

- express their own views freely and carefully attend to the expression of others' views
- propose and explore alternative ways of handling problems
- enter into role-playing activities enthusiastically
- describe, interpret, evaluate, and relate to their own lives what they see and hear in role-playing situations.

Suitability. This model emphasizes both personal growth and social interaction. It is most appropriate for use in social studies and literature, and is suitable for children in grades 3 through 8.

Considerations and precautions. The role-playing model requires that teachers present interpersonal situations which are amenable to several forms of resolution. Such situations must, of course, be interesting to the children and lie within their range of experience. The model also requires that teachers develop skills in managing role-playing situations. These may range from selecting and encouraging the "actors" to evaluating their presentations in terms of the ideas they put forward.

In choosing this model, teachers should clearly distinguish it both from psychodrama and from dramatics. They should focus on demonstration and discussion of interpersonal problem solving rather than on individual therapy or theatrical techniques.

B. Read the extended descriptions of the five models.

Each model is described at length in the second section of the book, "Five Teaching Models," beginning on page 63, and is organized in the following manner:

Introduction

PART 1 Classroom examples

PART 2 Procedures for using model-based instruction in the classroom

PART 3 Settings needed when using model-based instruction

PART 4 Anticipated student outcomes of using model-based instruction

PART 5 Checklists for evaluating a program based on the model

PART 6 References and resources

Appendix (first three models only)

As indicated earlier, each model is based on a set of assumptions about what children should learn and how such learning can be facilitated. Each description details the kinds of student learning you can expect in a program based on that model, provides prototype activities that are consonant with the model's assumptions, and includes probable pupil outcomes as well as guidelines for organizing instructional activities. After you've read the description of a teaching model, you'll want to think about its applicability to your individual situation. On the pages that follow, you will find questions to help you do this.

NOTE: If you are working in a planning team, use these questions as the basis for discussion and for becoming familiar with those models you are considering. If your intention is to produce a written program plan, be sure the person serving as recorder or secretary keeps a summary of the discussions.

Questions relating to a model's assumptions. Before answering the questions below, notice that the assumptions each model makes are listed in the Introduction and are implicit in the Anticipated Outcomes section as well as in the Checklist section.

• What kinds of decisions about how and what to learn do you intend to leave in the hands of the pupils? In your hands? What will you have to do to prepare your students to handle the decision making required of them by the model?

• How much content will come directly from you? From pupil interaction with peers? From individual study and activity? Can your classroom be arranged so that the pupils acquire information and develop skills in the ways suggested by the model?

• How structured should the learning materials be? Do you have ready access to appropriate materials?

• What conditions now in your classroom would facilitate model-related learning? Would impede it? Can you establish the necessary conditions?

Questions relating to student outcomes. It is useful to remember that the term "student outcomes" simply means the kinds of learning—cognitive, affective, and social—that are likely to result from students' experiences in the classroom. No matter what the model, student outcomes are stated at two levels of generality. The more general statements are potential program objectives—that is, the kinds of learning you might expect pupils to achieve by the end of the program, or the direction in which you expect pupils to move as a result of the program. (Obviously, a ten-week program cannot be expected to yield the same learning outcomes as a two-year program would. Also, some student learning outcomes may remain hidden for the present. Evidence that they have occurred may not surface until long after the program has ended.) The more specific statements describe sets of observable behaviors that contribute to program objectives.

Remember, too, that the second checklist is a source of anticipated pupil outcomes. These outcomes are stated in somewhat different form, since the purpose of the checklist is to note progress pupils make during the program.

Here are a number of questions to ask yourself concerning student outcomes:

• What constitutes progress on the part of the pupils?
• What specific information processing (if any) are emphasized in this model?

- Which interpersonal skills (if any) are emphasized?
- What specific feelings and attitudes (if any) does the model attempt to encourage?
- Which of these will be of specific concern to you?

Questions relating to model-based activities. Descriptions of activities include what the teacher does, what pupils do, the kinds of materials to be used, and how the classroom is organized. In planning model-based activities, you will need to establish criteria that can help you distinguish activities appropriate to the model from those that are not. In this connection, Parts 1, 2, 3, and 5 in the model description will be of particular use to you.

Be sure to read the classroom example(s). Do you feel you could conduct a lesson like this? How, if at all, would you modify or improve it?

Read, too, about the procedures and arrangements. Would you be able to do these things in your school? Would you modify or improve them?

Finally, look at Checklist 1. Do you agree with the characteristics of the activities as they are described on this list? Would you modify them?

To summarize your thoughts on model-based activities, ask yourself these questions:

- What are the essential characteristics of the learning activities included in this model?
- How do these activities differ from those I ordinarily use?
- What is it about these activities that can lead to the student outcomes I desire?

Questions relating to program organization. Organizing a program means sequencing the learning activities. You may want to arrange these activities in units according to the steps provided in the model, according to the subject matter, or in some other way. Parts 1, 2, and 3 of each model should be reviewed as you think about how to organize your own model-based program. Then ask yourself these questions:

- Can a sequence or preferred order for activities be inferred from the classroom example?
- Do the model's steps prescribe an instructional sequence?
- Do the characteristics of the activities require adherence to a particular sequence—either within an activity or between activities?
- Will the subject matter of your program influence or determine the sequence of activities? If so, is there any conflict between the sequencing of the subject matter and the model's requirements?

C. Become more informed about each of your likely models.

If you feel that you want to know more about a model before beginning to plan, consider the following suggestions:

1. *Search for additional written material about the models.* The best place to start is with the list of references and resources provided at the end of each model. Libraries likely to have the literature you are seeking are those associated with colleges and universities that have teacher preparation programs. Still other possibilities are curriculum and resource centers.

2. *Observe activities in existing model programs.* If a classroom or school is using activities similar to those in the model of interest to you, you might find it helpful to observe the pupils there and to speak with the teacher(s). To learn about such programs, you can

- ask fellow teachers
- call or write those in charge of curriculum development in your school district
- call or write to subject matter resource people
- contact a local teachers college or university
- locate curriculum materials that reflect a rationale similar to that of your model, and then write to the publishers to find out if these materials are being used in your area and, if so, where.

3. *Try out model-related activities in your own classroom.* If you want to gain personal experience with model-related activities, try out parts of the model before you begin to develop your program plan. You must keep in mind, however, that such a relatively limited experience will neither prove nor disprove the model's efficacy. What it *will* do is give you a feeling for how model ideas translate into classroom practices.

NOTE: If you are working in a planning team, the responsibilities for gathering information in this phase of your planning effort should be divided. For example, two people might do the library search; two others could locate classrooms where model-based activities are occurring; still others could design some activities to be tried out in your classroom.

Step 3: Program Planning

Overview of Step 3

A. Decide on the outcomes you expect students in your program to achieve.

B. Decide on the essential characteristics of the learning activities.

C. Decide on program organization.

D. Finalize your program plan.

A. Decide on the outcomes you expect students in your program to achieve.

Student outcomes can be stated at several levels of generality. The program objectives listed in Part 4 of the model descriptions are general statements which indicate what pupils can be expected to achieve by the end of the program. Each program objective should be supported, of course, by a set of related behaviors.

Begin by considering the program objectives included in your chosen model. Do you want to work with them? Revise them? Add others?

Here are some examples of model-based program objectives rewritten in such a way as to include specific content.

Example 1. Program objectives from an experiential learning model for a science program dealing with animals:

- Pupils will be able to classify animals in a variety of categories, such as their species, habitat, coloring, and eating habits.
- Pupils will be able to observe and describe accurately animal characteristics and behaviors.

Example 2. A program objective from a group inquiry model for a social studies program in American history:

- Pupils will be able to select a topic relevant to the American colonial experience and then plan to research it.

Example 3. A program objective from a creative thinking model for a language arts program emphasizing writing skills:

- Pupils will notice oddities in written material such as newspapers and magazines and will use them to generate ideas for writing fantasies.

Now look at the following tips related to writing objectives. Then use these tips to edit the objectives in your own model or else to make up new ones.

a. An objective should indicate what pupils will achieve, rather than what teachers will do. Writing an objective in this manner makes it possible to evaluate effectively the progress of your students.

b. An objective should be written in a general enough way so that many activities are required in order for pupils to accomplish it.

   c. An objective should be stated in such a manner that it conveys the same meaning to everyone who reads it. (Behaviors related to its achievement should be observable or measurable.)

   d. An objective should be made relevant to the teaching model used in organizing the program.

   e. An objective should be attainable by most pupils, given sufficient instruction. (It should *not* be an objective already achieved by most pupils *prior* to the instruction.)

Once you are satisfied with your general program objectives, you may wish to think of the sets of behaviors related to each one. Many teachers (and you may be one) don't want to take the time to break down and translate a program objective into sets of related behaviors. In this case, it is possible to develop learning activities directly from program objectives. However, the transition is easier if related student behaviors are listed first.

Related behaviors are pupil actions that show achievement of part or all of a program objective. Those behaviors listed in each model description are only suggestive; brainstorm for others, using the same format.

Here are some examples of model-based program objectives presented along with some specific related behaviors.

Example 1, program objective for a literature program using a role-playing model: Students will demonstrate their understanding of the motivation of characters in literature.

Related behaviors: Students will suggest several ideas about how a situation might be resolved; identify actions that suit one character more than another; think of possible consequences for a character following a particular course of action; explain why a proposed course of action fits or does not fit the situation.

Example 2, program objective for a poetry unit based on the concept analysis model: Students will demonstrate their understanding of the attributes of lyric poetry.

Related behaviors: When presented with an unfamiliar poem, students will identify it as a lyric poem; seek out and bring to class examples of different types of poetry for comparison; write one or more lyric poems; offer an interpretation of a lyric poem relating subject matter to style.

Example 3, program objective for an early childhood program based on an experiential learning model: Students will develop peer relationships that promote their own social and cognitive development.

Related behaviors: Students will be able to work cooperatively with children both older or younger than themselves; explain to one another how something works and thus receive instruction from one another; paraphrase the viewpoints of other children.

NOTE: If you are working in a planning team, the generation of objectives can be done collectively; or, to save time, individuals can assume responsibility for the first draft of one or more program objectives and related student behaviors. Critiquing and revising can then be done by the team as a whole.

Make sure to review the notes or minutes from previous meetings to see if they have relevance for this particular task.

B. Decide on the essential characteristics of the learning activities.

Learning activities are what your pupils will do—both inside and outside of the classroom—to achieve the program's objectives.

At this point, you obviously are *not* going to plan every single activity that will occur in your program. Nonetheless, it is important that you decide on the kinds of activities that will occur in the program and then develop criteria and prototypes for them. Well-described criteria can help you to generate additional activities that exhibit the essential characteristics of the teaching model.

Work then with the appropriate checklists or make your own list of criteria to which the learning activities must conform. You may come up with something like the following:

Activities using the creative thinking model should

- occur in a nonjudgmental atmosphere
- elicit a variety of student responses, solutions, and ideas
- encourage students to share their ideas
- allow students time to think about their ideas before being asked to respond to a question
- present students with ambiguous or unusual situations
- stimulate students to become good observers of detail
- encourage students to view situations from alternative perspectives.

As you develop your learning activities, check to see that they conform to most, if not all, of your stated criteria. These prototype activities could be summarized in a form similar to Figure 4.

This recommended form has a variety of useful features:

- It provides a way to key each activity to its objective.
- It calls attention to the sequence of activities, the materials employed, the instructional setting, and the need for other adults.
- It provides a space where both teacher and pupil reactions to an

Figure 4. Prototype Activity

The *name* of this activity is:

This activity will help students achieve the *program objective* that states:

Related behaviors elicited by this activity include:

The *procedures* (i.e., the steps taken by teachers and students) will be:

    Teacher procedures   *Student procedures*

The *arrangements* (e.g., time required; materials needed; instructional setting; adults needed) will be:

Comments (to be added after activity has been completed):

---

activity can be recorded. (Such information will help in evaluating and improving the activities. For example, if several teachers use and comment on a particular activity, those who have used it with success can be identified, and they can offer advice to others who were less satisfied with the outcome.)

However, whether you use this form or replace it with one of your own, be sure that the form you use meets two criteria:

• Activities should be described in such a way that others can understand them and anticipate what will happen in a classroom situation.
• They should reflect the model from which they are derived.

NOTE: If you are working in a planning team, list the activity characteristics jointly. To save time, team members can develop activity prototypes individually.

One basis for reviewing activity prototypes would be to use those characteristics previously agreed upon. After discussion, the team can then collect relevant instructional materials.

C. Decide on program organization.

You have already made many of the major decisions required by a new program. These include

- program emphasis
- the type and number of students in the program
- the approximate number of instructional hours required
- the program objectives, together with related student behaviors
- the characteristics of program activities.

It is now important that you anticipate *all* the tasks which must be done to bring your program into existence and to ensure that it is conducted efficiently. So, before the program begins, consider when to do some or all of the following:

- order materials
- reserve facilities
- schedule field trips
- hire aides
- solicit volunteers
- inform parents and others about the program
- organize and arrange furniture, books, bulletin boards, etc.
- schedule learning activities
- develop and use record-keeping systems to evaluate student progress.

A simple way to visualize all these tasks is a time line organized as in Figure 5. List the tasks in the left-hand column, and enter dates across the top row. For each task, make a dot under the beginning and ending dates, and then draw a horizontal line connecting them. Finally, add the name of the individual who is assigned the task.

A similar kind of time line to organize instruction during the program can also be easily constructed. The left-hand column might contain topics, or it might list objectives. The horizontal lines would indicate when activities related to those objectives would be carried out. Figure 6 provides an example of this type of time line.

NOTE: If you are working in a planning team, both the tasks and the schedule should be discussed with *all* those who will be involved in managing, teaching, or evaluating the program.

(Continued on page 46)

Figure 5. Task Time Line

Tasks to be done

1. _____

2. _____

3. _____

4. _____

5. _____

6. _____

7. _____

8. _____

9. _____

10. _____

11. _____

12. _____

(Enter weeks, months, or dates)

By whom

1. _____

2. _____

3. _____

4. _____

5. _____

6. _____

7. _____

8. _____

9. _____

10. _____

11. _____

12. _____

Figure 6. Objectives Time Line

	September				October				November					December				January			
	7	14	21	28	5	12	19	26	2	9	16	23	30	7	14	21	28	4	11	18	25
Obj. A. Pupils will learn that they are living during a time which has characteristics different from the past and the future.	↕																				
Obj. B. Pupils will begin to explore the backgrounds from which they come—cultural, ethnic, religious, etc.							↕														
Obj. C. Pupils will learn that traditions grow out of needs which are common to all people—the need for food, shelter, recreation, self-expression, etc.						↕							↕								
Obj. D. Pupils will become aware that people come from many different backgrounds.										↕					↕						
Obj. E. Pupils will learn to locate themselves within a geographic framework.														↕			↕				
Obj. F. Pupils will develop respect for and appreciation of their own traditions.			↕																↕		
Obj. G. Pupils will develop respect for and appreciation of the traditions of others.			↕																↕		

* Attitudinal student outcomes

If you have plans to continue or expand your program beyond its initial run, you will need to set aside time for revising it. The revisions should be based on your evaluation of its efficacy. Integrating the evaluation requirements with the program requirements will be discussed in Step 4.

D. Finalize your program plan.

A written description of your program can be important. It can serve as a common reference for everyone involved in teaching or administering it, and it can be useful when applying for special funding at some future date.

A program description usually has two parts: The first describes the program, and can be completed at this point; the second describes evaluation procedures and should be completed only after reading Step 4.

The outline you will find in Figure 7 lists major headings, indicates the questions which should be answered, and delineates the information needed to answer each question. (The sample program plan in the Appendix at the end of this book may be of help to you as you write your own plan.)

Step 4: Program Evaluation

Overview of Step 4

A. Decide on the evaluation questions you want to answer (1) for the program planning phase; (2) for the program revision phase; (3) for the program replication phase.
B. Decide on procedures for answering each evaluation question.
C. Develop an evaluation plan that is coordinated with your program plan.

A. Decide on the evaluation questions you want to answer.

Evaluations are conducted in order to collect data for answering questions that cannot easily be answered out of either past experience or intuition. Clearly, though, there is no single evaluation question or set of questions which constitute the "right" evaluation questions.

As a rule, questions for evaluation include:

• those which can be answered by using data collection techniques such as tests, questionnaires, interviews, observations, and records

Figure 7. Outline

Major Headings	Questions to Be Answered	Description of the Answer
1. IDENTIFYING INFORMATION	What kind of document is this?	Program name, name of school, principal, planning team members.
2. SUMMARY OF PROGRAM PLAN	What is in this document?	A short paragraph containing a one- or two-sentence description of each section.
3. DESCRIPTION OF PROGRAM AND RATIONALE FOR PLANNING IT	What are the goals of the program? Who are the intended users? Why was the program developed?	One or two paragraphs describing the goals of the program, its intended audience, and the reasons for developing it. (For example, pretesting may have revealed deficiencies in student achievement under the existing program; teachers or parents may have expressed a desire for a new program; or, perhaps, new knowledge within a subject field may require a new program.) Why this particular program was selected or developed should also be explained.
4. DESCRIPTION OF THE INSTRUCTIONAL COMPONENT	What are the areas in which pupil achievement is expected? What measurable student outcomes are anticipated? What activities will teachers be doing? Pupils be doing? How, with what materials, and when?	Description of program objectives with related behaviors; a summary of activities, materials, arrangements, and schedule.
5. ADMINISTRATIVE CHARACTERISTICS OF PROGRAM	What people and resources are to be used in this program? How much time will it take? What will be the cost?	Description of pupils served (number and reason for inclusion, such as age, grade, interest, need, etc.); resources needed, such as space (classrooms, other facilities), staff (teachers, aides, volunteers, etc.), equipment, or materials; time (duration and amount); budget (divided into initial expenses and maintenance expenses).
6. DESCRIPTION OF THE EVALUATION	How will the program be evaluated? What questions will be asked? What measures will be taken? How will data be analyzed and interpreted?	Description of purpose of evaluation (the questions which the evaluation will answer); design of evaluation; methods and measures to be used (the tests, records, or reports) for collecting information; method of analysis (the ways in which information is to be organized and interpreted); schedule for evaluation.
7. DESCRIPTION OF THE MANAGEMENT COMPONENT	When and by whom will the instruction and evaluation be carried out?	Description of program schedule (i.e., time line).

- those about which there is some uncertainty as to the answer
- those which must be answered in order to make program-related decisions
- those which are important to answer because they are of concern to a number of people
- those to which answers are required by funding agencies.

It has become conventional within the world of program evaluation to ask questions about students' knowledge, skills, or attitudes before the program begins, at several points during the program, once the program is completed, and perhaps, at some point six months or a year after the program has ended.

It has likewise become commonplace to collect evaluation information about program processes. These may be framed in terms of such administrative details as the type(s) of students served, the amount of time spent on program activities, the books and equipment used, student-teacher transactions, and teaching-learning activities. In any case, when using a model-based program, the teacher's documentation of program processes should be based on the essential characteristics of the teaching model he or she has chosen.

The conventional reason for asking questions about student learning and program processes at several points in time is that this procedure provides boundaries for thinking about what to evaluate. However, if teachers are faithful to our definition of evaluation (i.e., the systematic selection, collection, and interpretation of information to be used in decision making), then any evaluation question which conforms to the five points listed above is appropriate.

From a practical point of view, the three critical times when evaluation can inform decision making occur while the program is being conceptualized, during its first series of trial runs, and once the program has been established and taught a few times.

While the program is being conceptualized or planned, it is important for you to collect preassessment data about the students who are likely to be in the program. Such data will influence

- the way in which you describe your program objectives and related student behaviors
- the materials and activities you will assemble in order to have students achieve the program objectives and demonstrate the related behaviors
- the sequencing of activities
- the amount of time you will allocate for students to move toward the achievement of program objectives.

While the program is being taught for the first or second time, collecting evaluation data will help you

- keep track of changes in the students' knowledge, skills, and attitudes
- document actual, rather than intended, program activities
- revise activities that do not promote the hoped-for student learning.

After the program has become established, evaluation data will be useful for

- assuring the program's continued existence as part of the ongoing school offering
- documenting both processes and outcomes for other teachers who may wish to adopt the program.

It might seem premature to you to be asked to consider evaluation questions when you are just beginning to formulate the program. However, a little thought at this point can have both immediate and long-term payoffs. First, the intellectual exercise of considering which evaluation questions to answer will sharpen your understanding of *what* you want to do in the program as well as *how* to do it in the best way possible. Second, you will better understand that resources in the form of time, money, and skill must be set aside for answering the evaluation questions. Third, a written evaluation plan—even if not highly formalized or fine-tuned—provides reassurance for you, the program developer, that a self-monitoring system is in place. Fourth, it will be persuasive to others who wish to learn more about your program. And, finally, it is an absolute necessity if at some point you intend to apply for funds to disseminate your program beyond your immediate circle of colleagues.

1. *Possible evaluation questions to answer for the program-planning phase.* The three steps in the planning agenda that you have already read through—thinking about the kind of program you want, selecting a teaching model, and building a model-based program—draw heavily on one's creativity. After all, you are bringing into existence a completely new entity. Evaluating this new entity against actual student needs can be done by asking the following questions:

- What behaviors do students currently exhibit in relation to each of your proposed program objectives? (The answer to this question should modify the way you frame your program objectives and the behaviors that you associate with them.)
- What are the current attitudes of students in relation to proposed

model-based learning activities? (The answer to this question should help you better estimate how to introduce and sequence the learning activities.)

• Are there identifiable differences among students in terms of their readiness to participate in the program? (The answer to this question will indicate the extent to which you must individualize your instruction.)

2. *Possible evaluation questions to answer for the program revision phase.* Creating an integrated, model-based educational program is a demanding task requiring flexibility. No one can be certain in advance of all of the difficulties, activities, or events that will occur as a program develops. Nor can anyone know in advance whether it is possible or desirable to translate all the ideas from paper into practice. As you teach, however, you will be in a position to revise your plan. You will very quickly become aware that some activities simply don't work, or that those which do work require a very different treatment from the ones you had anticipated. The decision about what to maintain, what to add, and what to drop in a program can be implemented by collecting information in advance on the following points:

• Have the procedures for using the model been followed?
• Have the arrangements for using the model been implemented?
• How much time has been allocated to model-based instructional activities?
• What attitudes do teachers have about the model-based activities?
• What successes/difficulties have previous teachers had in using model-based activities?
• How much time have students actually spent engaged in activities that contain essential model-related characteristics?
• Have these students experienced success with the model-based activities?
• What attitudes did students bring to such activities?
• What varying behaviors did they exhibit in relation to program objectives at various times during the program?

3. *Possible evaluation questions to answer for the program-replication phase.* At this point, it may well be that you do not anticipate having the program taught by teachers other than those who were involved in its initial planning. On the other hand, you may be expecting your program to be so effective and so enthusiastically received that you will readily be able to persuade others to undertake similar efforts. If the former is true, you should not concern yourself with the questions on page 51. In the latter case, however, you should answer those questions and read this section with particular care. Understanding just how monies are awarded for

dissemination of innovative programs may be of critical importance.

Since the early 1970s, federal and state agencies concerned with education have been very interested in getting good innovative programs known outside their originating sites. Toward this end, they have made funds available for dissemination activities. Eligibility to apply for such funds has been made contingent upon the submitting of evidence that the program has been effective. Although it is not feasible here to provide you with a complete description of what is necessary by way of evaluative data, the following brief overview should be helpful.

State requirements differ, but most of them are modeled on the federal system. This system works something like this: There is a Joint Dissemination Review Panel (JDRP) composed of representatives from a number of government agencies concerned with education. These panel members decide whether your program and its evaluation meet the necessary standards for effectiveness. Their decision is based upon a document of approximately ten pages which you have to write and submit to the panel, as well as upon your oral presentation. The written part of this submission must include a brief description of the project, as well as its goals and objectives. It must indicate the setting in which the project has occurred, the types of students served, a program description of essential activities or program components, and a list of materials used. The costs of the program must also be specified. All of these elements have already been described in your written program plan.

An equally important part of this submission, however, is evidence of the effectiveness of the program. Not only must student learning be documented, but evaluation data must already exist so that the panel can be reasonably confident that any gains in the students' knowledge, skills, or attitudes can be directly attributed to the program rather than to normal maturation, the ongoing educational process, or some other outside factor. In short, the panel wants some concrete, reliable measure or estimate of what would have happened to the students if they had *not* been in the program.

Some examples of the evaluation questions that need to be answered if funds for program replication are to be obtained are the following:

- What kinds of student knowledge, skills, behavior, and attitudes can be uniquely associated with the program?
- What evidence is there indicating that students changed in terms of their knowledge, skills, behaviors, and attitudes?
- What evidence is there that these student outcomes can be attributed to the program rather than to some other cause?
- What evidence is there that the program will work as successfully with students in other settings?

B. Decide on procedures for answering each evaluation question.

If you have not had experience in designing or developing evaluation instruments, you should seriously consider hiring a consultant who will advise you on how to do this. You may also want to refer to the material contained in the *CSE Program Evaluation Kit.*[7] In designing any evaluative instrument, there are a number of places where technical knowledge is necessary, especially for collecting data to answer the evaluative questions connected with the program replication phase. Space is lacking here to provide you with complete details on how to carry out an evaluation. Instead, what we propose to do is to alert you to certain basic evaluation considerations.

Too often, "evaluation" has been elevated—by both those within and those outside the field—into a mystical and somewhat arcane art form. It is nothing of the kind though. Evaluation is simply a systematic way of collecting data with instruments that are open to public inspection, and of using design and analytic procedures that can be replicated by other investigators. A less systematic or more informal data collection process can be useful in cases where you quickly want to learn more than you currently know, or when you want to track complex events as they occur over time. Informal data collection can also give you a better picture of the dynamics of a program than can the more circumscribed "temperature-taking" generally associated with the intermittent administration of tests and other measures. The formality of an evaluation—including the need to establish the validity and reliability of the evaluation instruments—increases in proportion to the demands for highly credible and certain data. For example, if you want to target more precisely your program objectives for a particular group of students, you might first talk to some of them, watch them in classrooms, interview their current teachers, and look at their test scores. However, these informal methods would be unsatisfactory if you were collecting, for example, preprogram data to compare with postprogram data as a way of making assertions about program effectiveness.

In short, conduct "do-it-yourself" informal data collecting when you want to supplement already available information, or when you want to get an intimate sense of program activities and student changes over time. Get professional and/or technical assistance, though, when you need evaluative data that will withstand external scrutiny or support your request for expensive high-risk decisions.

In Figure 8, you will find a number of methods and instruments, both formal and informal, that can effectively be used to collect evaluative data.

As you think about the instruments you will use to collect data to

Figure 8. Data Collecting

Instruments for Collecting Data

About student knowledge

Formal:
- currently available norm- or criterion-referenced written tests which use formats such as short answer, multiple choice, matching, or essay
- general tests or curriculum-embedded tests
- oral examination with standardized questions and standardized rating criteria.

Informal:
- teacher-developed quizzes
- conversations with students
- observation of how students interact with one another
- written assignments or other class work
- informal anecdotal records (kept by teachers).

About student skills or behaviors

Formal:
- oral or written tests designed to elicit a specific skill or behavior
- structured observation of student performance in role-playing settings
- structured observation in normal settings
- rating of assignments or work products (using rating criteria).

Informal:
- nonstructured observation of student performance in normal classroom settings
- occasional examination of written assignments or other class work.

About student attitudes

Formal:
- written responses to questionnaires using such formats as checklists, rankings, ratings, Q sorts, semantic differentials, forced choice, open-ended questions, etc.
- structured or semistructured interviews with students
- structured or semistructured observations that tally frequency, duration, or intensity of behaviors in normal classroom settings
- teacher logs (with specified entries)
- examination of records (absence, tardiness, number of books checked out of library, etc.).

(Continued)

Figure 8 (continued)

Informal:
- conversations with parents and other teachers
- conversations with students
- unplanned observations
- teacher diaries (with occasional anecdotal entries or critical incidents).

About use of model-based procedures and arrangements

Formal:
- observation schedules (based on model checklist)
- interviews (based on model checklist)
- teacher logs (with specified entries)
- questionnaires (relating to use of model procedures).

Informal:
- conversations with teachers
- occasional classroom observations.

About time allocated to model-based activities

Formal:
- teacher logs (with specified entries)
- tabulations (of daily lesson plans).

Informal:
- teacher estimates (on daily, weekly, or program basis).

About teacher attitudes toward model-based activities

Formal:
- written responses to questionnaires using various formats (see "About student attitudes" above)
- structured interviews.

Informal:
- conversations with teachers
- inferences from occasional observations or incidents.

About teacher successes/difficulties

Formal:
- questionnaires
- interviews
- structured observations.

Figure 8 (continued)

Informal:
- conversations
- occasional observations.

About student-engaged time

Formal:
- records (with specified entries)
- structured observations.

Informal:
- conversations with teachers and students
- occasional observations.

About student successes/difficulties

Formal:
- examination of student work
- interviews with students
- structured observations.

Informal:
- conversations with students
- occasional observations.

---

answer your evaluation questions, you must think about *who* will be the respondents. The teachers in the program are one obvious choice for answering evaluation questions relating to program processes. Students in the program—either all of them or a random sample—are also appropriate respondents, especially for finding out what the effects of the program are. (For evaluation questions related to the program-planning phase or to the program-revision phase, it is unlikely that you will want to approach students outside the program. This is especially true if you have decided on informal, rather than formal methods of collecting data.)

Sometimes, in the case of evaluations that are related to the program-replication phase, students in other programs may have to be called upon as respondents. If this proves necessary, the procedures in Figure 9, which indicate both who the respondents are and the times allocated for collecting data, will give you a brief idea of the choices available to you when conducting a formal evaluation. Once again though, we caution you *not* to try to set up a formal evaluation design on your own without consulting the *CSE Program Evaluation Kit,* examining other texts, or calling in an experienced consultant.

Figure 9. Procedures for Collecting Data

Respondents and Times

Experimental group only: pretest-posttest. A pretest-posttest design uses the same or parallel forms of one or more formal tests or measures of knowledge, skills and/or behaviors, and/or attitudes.

Unfortunately, with this design it is impossible to say with certainty that any before/after changes in students' knowledge, skills, or attitudes are due specifically to the program; there are a host of other possible explanations. For example, normal maturation may account for the gains, or else nonschool-related experiences may have resulted in increased learning.

Experimental group and true control group: pretest-posttest. If you use this design, pupils are randomly assigned to your program, to an alternative program, or to no program at all. The distinguishing feature in this procedure is that pupils have been *randomly* assigned. This means that the names of all second-graders, for instance, are put into a hat; then half of the names drawn are assigned to the program while the other half are assigned to an alternate one. Assigning pupils in such a random way ensures that the two groups are similar to one another at the start of the program and that, therefore, the student results in your program can be determined (by pre- and posttest) to be directly due to that program. In other words, if pupils assigned to the program surpass pupils in an alternative program or in no program, you have good reason to assume that the program itself contributed to this result. However, if you use just one class, each, of experimental and "control group," you must also consider the effects of the *teacher* on the students. In so doing, document what both the "experimental" program and the "other" program were.

Experimental group and true control group: posttest only. This design is the same as the preceding one, except that it excludes the pretest(s). It is preferred in situations where the pretest(s) might affect learning, or where it is impossible to give them.

Experimental group and nonequivalent control group: pretest-posttest. In this design, already existing groups of pupils, or classes, can be compared with one another to determine the effects of your program as against those of an alternative program. The use of this design assumes that the two groups of pupils compared are roughly equivalent to one another at the start of each program.

Figure 9 (continued)

Unfortunately, this is often an assumption difficult to substantiate. Therefore, pre-measures indicating that the groups are similar to one another are helpful. In addition, there are a variety of statistical techniques which can equate the postprogram performance of both groups if the differences in their preprogram performance are known. If the extent of their preprogram similarity is unknown, it is almost impossible to attribute any postprogram differences among students to a particular program rather than to other factors.

Since this design calls for assigning classes rather than individual pupils to alternate programs, it is often easier to implement than a true control group design would be. Though this design can yield useful comparative information, any causal inferences about program effects must be made with extreme caution.

Experimental group only: time series.   A time series design does not require a "control group" in order to get comparative information, since the group of pupils within the program serve as their own controls. Instead of providing a comparison between the performance of pupils in your program and pupils in some other program (or in no program at all), this design provides you with a comparison between pupils' performance in the chosen program and what might have been predicted about their performance had they continued learning as they had previously learned. To use this design, it is necessary to have at least three scores on the same measure for the same child, taken at some regular interval prior to the beginning of the program. An additional score on that measure must then be obtained at the end of the program. In this way, it can be statistically determined whether or not pupils in the program exceeded, met, or fell below what might have been expected of them given their previous scores.

Experimental groups and other comparison groups.   A *cohort group* differs from an *experimental group* in that it consists of students similar to those in a nonequivalent control group, except for the fact that they have had their educational experiences *at an earlier time* than the experimental group did.

A *norm group* consists of students similar to those in a nonequivalent control group, except for the fact that they have had their educational experiences *in a setting different from the one for the experimental group.*

Using this design requires that the experimental group and the comparison group—whether it be cohort or norm—be as similar to one another as possible, and that the similarities, as well as the differences, be documented. It also requires that the same data collection instruments be administered to both groups at approximately the same points in time. Since there are many statistical problems associated with analyzing this type of data, getting expert assistance is advisable.

C. Develop an evaluation plan that is coordinated with your program plan.

An effective evaluation plan should include a description of the following:

- evaluation questions to be answered
- instruments to be used
- respondents—teachers, students, parents, etc.
- times for collecting information
- costs of collecting information
- schedule for tasks/time/personnel.

There is no single layout or procedure which is the ultimate in convenience for displaying the coordinated program information and the evaluation information. The sample program and evaluation plan in the Appendix at the end of this book represents one informal way of presenting the program and evaluation interface. Still another method is to use a separate form for the evaluation plan and then to draw up a coordinated program evaluation calendar. A layout for an evaluation plan is presented in Figure 10.

Following is a quick review of material that will help you complete each element (*a* through *h*) in Figure 10.

a. • Decide on which questions you are using in this plan, and then employ a separate form for each question.
    • Look over the possible questions we have suggested in connection with each phase (see pages 49–52). Filter each of these questions by asking: "Will the planning, teaching, or revising of the program change if the answer to this question is X rather than Y?" *Only select those evaluative questions that you know will influence your decision making.* But what if none of the questions we have supplied are useful to you? Generate your own, then by asking yourself: "What program decisions am I uncertain about?" "Can I learn anything that will help to reduce this uncertainty?"
    • Do not attempt to answer more than two or three evaluative questions in connection with each phase.

b. Respondents here may be either teachers or students. For the *planning* or *revision* phases, they will be individuals or groups in the program; for the program *replication* phase, they may include other individuals or groups.

c. The instruments for collecting information may be either informal or formal during the first two phases. For the third phase, you will probably want to use formal instruments. Review our suggestions; then generate your own informal instruments.

Figure 10. Layout for an Evaluation Plan

Evaluation Plan for _____   Program Name _____

(a)
Evaluative question(s)
to be answered

(b)
Respondents
will be

(c)
Instruments for collecting
information will be

(d)
Times for collecting
information will be

(e)
Costs for collecting
information will be

Salaries
Printing &
Production
Purchase of
instruments
Travel
Data analysis
Other
TOTAL

(f)
Tasks to be done

(g)
When (enter the starting and ending dates)
Week 1 2 3 4 5 6 7 8 9 10 etc.

(h)
By whom

d. Times for collecting information are likely to occur at the following intervals: before the program begins; after specific units are completed; at regular intervals during the year (i.e., mid-semester), and at the end of the program. For the third phase, follow-up data is useful to have at six-month or yearly intervals.

e. Costs for collecting information can be computed in a number of ways. If a consultant is available to help, let that individual estimate his or her costs. If you must do it
   • list tasks to be done (f) and by whom (h)
   • estimate number of hours spent by each person
   • multiply hours by individual's salary rate
   • add all salary costs together
   • estimate other expenses (be generous in your time allocations; things usually take longer than expected).

f. Some of the tasks typically associated with an evaluation are
   • deciding on evaluation questions
   • choosing respondents
   • deciding on types of instruments
   • selecting instruments
   • developing instruments
   • training people in the use of these instruments
   • scheduling data collection time
   • establishing filing system
   • distributing instruments
   • verifying that all respondents have completed procedures
   • storing data
   • training analysts (if necessary)
   • analyzing data
   • interpreting data
   • providing feedback to appropriate groups and/or individuals
   • making decisions.

g. Enter the beginning and ending times for each activity by making a dot under the appropriate week. Then connect the dots. By doing this you can easily see how activities overlap.

h. Indicate the name(s) of the responsible individual(s).

FIVE TEACHING MODELS

4
The Concept
Analysis Model

This model[1] provides pupils with orderly, systematic instruction in processing information. It assumes that, as pupils learn to conceptualize and make sense of their environment, they should receive instruction in classification and discrimination skills. They should also be taught a body of important concepts that will enable them to deal with their environment and to communicate with others.

Introduction

PART 1.   Classroom Examples

PART 2.   Procedures for Using the Concept Analysis Model in the Classroom

PART 3.   Settings Needed When Using the Concept Analysis Model

PART 4.   Anticipated Student Outcomes of Using the Concept Analysis Model

PART 5.   Checklists for Evaluating a Program Based on the Concept Analysis Model

PART 6.   References and Resources

Appendix

Introduction

The concept analysis model addresses itself to the task of helping children to develop skills for processing information, classification, and discrimination. This chapter also provides suggestions for selecting important concepts to be taught within a subject area, analyzing them, and then presenting them to students in the most efficient way.

Many teachers and parents see the development of conceptual skills as the primary goal of education because they recognize that these skills enable children to make sense of their environment and to communicate clearly. They believe too, that such skills can and should be systematically taught, starting with the pupil's first experiences in school.

Various investigators in the fields of psychology and education have explored the questions of how children conceptualize their world and how they can be helped to improve their classification skills. In this model, the works of the following researchers have been interpreted so that they will have application in the classroom: Peter Martorella,[2] Jean Piaget,[3] and Hilda Taba.[4]

In the pages that follow, the term "concept" will be defined and explained. Two other important issues that will be addressed are how children develop concepts and how such concepts can be taught efficiently. Finally, the theoretical assumptions which underlie the model will also be presented.

What is a concept?

Although there are many definitions of the term "concept," we shall define it here as a category or a construct that comes into being as one organizes his/her perceptions and experiences. The word "construct" is used advisedly, since the process of developing and attaining a concept can be thought of as a construction process—the putting together of separate pieces of information into meaningful entities. Of course, the assortment of information put together in the process of developing a concept is unique to each individual. The astronaut who has walked upon the surface of the moon has one concept of "moon"; an astronomer has another; and those of us who occasionally glance up at it in the evening sky hold yet another. Usually, however, people are sufficiently agreed on the critical attributes of a concept so that communication can occur among them.

A concept is not a concrete entity that can be seen or touched; rather, it is an organizer. A toddler in the process of "organizing" his world might refer to all four-legged animals—dogs, cats, horses, cows—as "doggie."

While his current organization of the world permits him to distinguish between people and animals, it does not help him to make a distinction between dogs and nondogs. Similarly, while he may have a concept of "dog," it just does not happen to coincide with the adult concept of "dog."

Peter Martorella suggests that for instructional purposes a concept "may be thought of as a category of experience having a *rule* which defines the relevant category, a set of *positive instances* or *exemplars* with *attributes* and a *name*." He defines these terms as follows:

NAMES   "Symbols commonly used by a culture to identify or label a concept" (e.g., a parallelogram)

RULE   "The definition or formula specifying the attributes of a concept" (e.g., a four-sided figure, the opposite sides of which are parallel and equal in length)

ATTRIBUTES   "Those characteristics which are the identifying features of a concept, and which enable one to distinguish between exemplars and non-exemplars" (e.g., four sides, opposite sides parallel, opposite sides equal in length)

EXEMPLARS   "Positive instances [or examples] of the concept; non-exemplars [are] negative examples lacking one or more of the necessary attributes" [5]

exemplars:

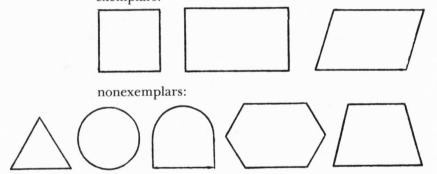

nonexemplars:

Concept name. Children as well as adults are frequently able to use a concept name without understanding the concept itself. This deficiency is particularly commonplace in a classroom where assessment procedures are used which depend exclusively upon the pupils' ability to provide the most appropriate words when explaining something. For example, a teacher who wishes to find out what the pupils know about political systems may discover that they may use the word "democracy" correctly in describing the American political system, and are even able, perhaps, to identify one attribute of democracy: people elect their own representatives. But, by questioning them further, the teacher may well discover that they are *not* able to identify any additional attributes, or to distinguish between exemplars and nonexemplars—even when given relevant information. Consequently, you should be careful not to accept concept names—even when used in the proper context—as proof in itself of concept mastery.

It is possible to err in the opposite direction also. A child may understand a concept without knowing the name of the concept. For example, a second grader who has been avidly reading books of all kinds since she was five years old can probably distinguish between those that are fiction and those that are nonfiction. Yet she may not know the *names* of these categories.

Concept rule. Concepts vary in the specificity of their rules or definitions. Some concepts are clearly defined by law or by scientific convention, and there is very little room for personal interpretation. With such concepts, it is possible to use the rule or definition to examine and identify exemplars. For example, given the definition of a parallelogram and an understanding of the concepts contained within it (i.e., parallel sides, opposites, etc.), a pupil can examine any geometric shape and determine if it is or is not a parallelogram. On the other hand, the rules or definitions of many nonmathematical, nonscientific concepts may fail to provide clear guidelines. Consider, for example, the concept "slang." Two of the important attributes of a word considered to be slang are that its use is short-lived, and that it is used by a particular group within the society, rather than by the society as a whole. Thus, the word "jazz," which began as slang, ceased to be slang when it gained widespread usage and proved to be an enduring term. On the other hand, the verb form "ain't" continues to be regarded as a slang term, even though it exhibits only one of the supposedly critical attributes of slang.

There are also concepts which have rules that provide few, if any, guidelines for distinguishing exemplars from nonexemplars. For example, concepts like excellence, honor, and integrity are highly dependent upon personal interpretation.

Concept attributes. The attributes of a concept are those features by which a concept can be identified. Although every concept has a multitude of attributes, not all of them are critical—that is, not all of them must be present in order for the concept to exist. Thus, the attributes of the concept "school" for a nursery school child might include such things as swings and slides. But these are not critical attributes of the concept "school" in general, even though they are attributes of the child's particular school. One can certainly have a school without swings and slides. The critical attributes of the general concept "school" are those attributes without which one would not have a school—namely, teachers and pupils.

To identify adequately the attributes of a concept, one must be able to list *all* of the critical attributes, group them in sets, and/or recognize and describe a particular relationship among them. Jerome Bruner and his colleagues categorize concepts according to the three ways in which their attributes define them:

1. "Concepts that are defined by the joint presence of [specific] attributes" (e.g., dog: animal, meat-eating, fur-covered, four-legged, etc.)
2. Concepts that are defined by the presence of one or the other of two or more sets of attributes (e.g., a strike in baseball: a ball swung at and missed, or a ball not swung at but passing over the plate between the shoulders and knees of the batter. In other words, two or more sets of attributes are needed here to explain a strike.)
3. Concepts that are "defined by a specifiable relationship [among the] attributes"[6] (e.g., pet: an animal kept by a person for the purposes of companionship and amusement).

Young children tend to focus on just one attribute of an object at a time; therefore, concepts that require attention not only to sets of attributes but also to the relationships among these attributes tend to be especially difficult for them to grasp.

Concept exemplars. Concepts vary in the ease with which their exemplars can be identified. Some concepts, such as "dog," "pet," and "cloud," have concrete exemplars about which there can be little disagreement. Others, like "democracy" and "justice," are far more abstract constructs and so can engender considerable disagreement.

Although you may not be interested in teaching such abstract concepts as "democracy" to a first grader, you may want to introduce them to elementary school children in the upper grades. In such an event, your goal will obviously be something less than complete mastery, since mastery implies that students would be able to identify exemplars *every* time they encountered them.

Concept development in children

Children learn concepts by organizing their perceptions of the world around them. They develop, for example, a concept of "dog" based on multiple encounters with such entities—dogs of various sizes, breeds, shapes, and colors. In turn, they become able to recognize the crucial attributes of "dog" and can then look at any animal and decide whether or not it is a dog.

Concept development in children is hierarchical and cumulative. Children must be able to grasp concepts like "dog" and "cat" before they attain the concept "animal," because the latter includes the concepts "dog," "cat," etc.

As mentioned earlier, young children have particular difficulty with concepts involving relationships. Piaget explains this by pointing out that children have difficulty entertaining two points of view simultaneously. Given a concept like "enemy," for example, they will often fail to recognize its reciprocal nature: Not only is one an enemy to one's enemy, but all those qualities attributed to the enemy are simultaneously attributable to oneself by one's enemy.

Children also tend to think in terms of absolutes. A dog is always a dog; an animal is always an animal. But, when today's pet chicken loses its status as pet and ends up as tomorrow's dinner, the young child cannot understand why. (For a more extensive explanation of how, according to the developmental theory of Piaget, the thinking of children differs from the thinking of adults, see the Appendix of this model, page 95, and the Appendix of the experiential learning model, page 158.)

Young children also have difficulty with abstract concepts. Although the concept "pet" might be more difficult for a child to grasp than the concept "dog," pet does have concrete referents or exemplars. For example, one can point to a pet in the same way that one can point to a dog or other animal; similarly, one can make clear distinctions between animals that function as pets and those that do not. However, the same cannot be said for abstract concepts like "honesty" and "friendship," which frequently engender disagreements (even among adults) as to their defining attributes and their exemplars.

Consider the following example of a woman who felt that her son had done something unethical. She had discovered that her six-year-old son was selling one of his old toys to his favorite playmate for ten times what the toy had originally cost. The buyer, naturally, was delighted to purchase the toy and even had the money to pay for it. The seller was delighted to receive the money. Everyone was delighted, in fact, except the mother, who was hard pressed to find a clear way of explaining her discomfort with this transaction to the two children. As she spoke with them, though, she discovered that the only economic concept they understood was that of "money" as a commodity exchangeable for goods. However, they had no knowledge of "profit" (let alone *excess* profit), nor did they have any more than a primitive understanding of the relative value of a penny and a dime. In addition, they did not understand her appeal to the rules of friendship, or consider the transaction an unfriendly act, since both were well satisfied with the resultant exchange. Finally, she had to give up and allow the transaction to stand. "Ethics," "excess profit," "friendship constraints"—all these concepts were simply too difficult to explain to a pair of contented six-year-olds.

Much of a child's conceptual development occurs informally and unsystematically. Thus it is not uncommon for a child to have learned to use a concept label correctly but to have only partially—or even erroneously—learned the attributes of that concept. An eight-year-old, for example, startled his mother when he revealed to her his embarrassment at having to tell his friends that she was returning to school. (She was planning to complete her college education, which had been interrupted by the birth of her children.) To him, school was a place just for children.

Even adults may vary in their understanding of concepts. Many people have heard of DNA molecules. But how many who are untrained in the sciences can do more than use the term in its proper context? For most adults, there is no great necessity to master this concept unless, of course, they wish to grapple with other concepts that depend upon such a mastery.

Every day in classrooms teachers ask their students to grapple with concepts that depend upon the mastery of other concepts. It is important, therefore, that teachers attempt to help children master basic concepts in as clear and systematic a way as possible. If children are to learn important concepts thoroughly, the teacher must

- clearly identify these concepts
- examine them carefully beforehand to identify likely sources of confusion
- determine what previous learning the children must have had before they can be presented with the new concepts
- sequence the instruction logically in order to facilitate the learning process
- devise adequate ways of finding out (both before and after the instruction period) whether or not the children have mastered the concepts in question.

Assumptions of the concept analysis model

1. Children can and should be instructed in developing classification and discrimination skills that will help them to process information.

2. Children can and should be taught, in systematic fashion, important concepts that are essential to basic subject matter disciplines.
3. Instruction in concept formation and concept attainment can and should be part of a child's first experiences in school.
4. In selecting concepts, designing an instructional plan for teaching them, and evaluating appropriately the success of the learning episode, teachers must remember the following assumptions:
   a. A child's grasp of a concept is highly dependent upon his/her own personal and direct experiences with the concept.
   b. Young children tend to have difficulty with abstract concepts or concepts that involve relationships.
   c. The fact that a child may use a concept name appropriately does not necessarily mean that he or she understands the concept.
   d. Children may have learned a concept without necessarily knowing the generally accepted name for that concept.

Part 1: Classroom Examples

Example 1 [7]

Mr. Brown's third-grade class has been working on a science unit, *Material Objects*, which introduces the children to the basic concepts of objects and their properties. Two of the major objectives of this unit are to teach children to recognize material objects common to their environment and then to help them distinguish the objects themselves from their properties. Up until now the children have had the opportunity to examine the various properties of many different objects. Today, Mr. Brown plans to introduce to them the concept of "material composition." He is going to ask them to describe and sort a collection of objects according to their material composition, and then to distinguish between objects made of one material and those made of more than one material.

Pupils are provided with concrete examples that can be seen, touched, felt, etc.

Mr. Brown asks the children to gather around a demonstration table on which are arrayed a number of objects, each of which is composed of a specific material. Some of the objects are rectangular bars provided in the science kit; others are household objects or pieces of objects, such as broom handles, a beer can, toothpicks, brass doorknobs, etc. He has chosen this varied group of objects so that the children will not focus on just size or shape as attributes of material composition.

He begins the lesson as follows:

MR. B: This (pointing to a word on the board) is the word "material." Say the word with me.

CLASS: Material.

SUSIE: That's what my mommy uses to make my dresses.

MR. B: You're right, Susie. That's one meaning for the word "material." But we can use this word in another way—to describe what any object is made of. Another word for what your mother uses to make your dresses is "cloth." My socks are made of cloth. But is this table made of cloth?

An attempt is made to reduce distractors (in this case, irrelevant attributes).

CLASS (shouts from around the table: No! It's made of wood.

MR. B: Right, this table is made of a material that we call wood. Now, is that windowpane made of a material?

CLASS: Yes!

MR. B: What material is the pane of that window made of?

CLASS (shouts from around the table): Glass!

Pupils are encouraged to develop skills of observation and description.

MR. B: Right. You all catch on very quickly. Now, let's look at these objects on the table. They all are made of some material. Touch them; feel them. Tell me in what ways they are alike.

(A discussion ensues in which the children talk about the similarities of the objects and describe them in terms of such things as shape, color, feel, etc.)

MR B (continuing): Now, let me show you some of the differences in these objects.

(Using a knife, he cuts off pieces of the wood and polystyrene objects and shows the class that these objects have different consistencies. He uses a rasp to scrape the surface of the brass object. He tells them that materials are given names because they look and feel different from one another. He now sets out an assortment of cards, each one bearing the name of one of the materials corresponding to the sample objects—i.e., brass, wood, vinyl, polystyrene, aluminum. He then reads the label names and tells the class to help him place each object in a group, according to the material it is made of. When he is done, he says that each group now contains objects made of just one material.)

MR. B (holding up a pencil):   Can I put the pencil in one of these groups?

CLASS: No . . . It doesn't go . . . It has an eraser . . . (etc.).

MR. B: Right. I can't put the pencil in one of these groups because different parts of the pencil are made of different materials. Now, how many materials do you think this pencil is made of?

(He demonstrates the composition of the pencil by identifying the rubber eraser, by scraping off the paint to show the wood underneath, by scraping some of the graphite from the point, etc. He then places a new

---

Pupils are provided with a variety of exemplars and nonexemplars simultaneously.

---

assortment of objects on the table and encourages the children to handle and examine them. Some are made of one material; some, of more than one. He then holds up another label which reads "more than one material" and asks the children to help him group the new items. He calls on each child to select the group to which the item belongs.)

Pupils are asked to explain their reasoning processes.

MR. B: Why do *you* think it belongs in the group? (Then after all the items have been categorized in this way): Now, who can tell me again what the word "material" means?

SEVERAL CHILDREN (volunteering):   It's what things are made of.

Information to be learned is related to each pupil's experience.

Finally, Mr. Brown concludes the lesson by asking each child to bring two objects to school the next day—one made of just one material, and another made of more than one material—so that, together, they can construct a "Materials Museum."

Example 2 [8]

Ms. Crenshaw's fourth- and fifth-grade class is studying about village life in Serbia, a state in Yugoslavia. This week she has introduced the children to the concept of "tradition."

She begins by asking them to read a story and shows them some pictures. Both the story and the pictures have to do with a Yugoslavian family's preparation for a special feast day called the Slava and their

---

Pupils are encouraged to develop skills of observation and description.

---

celebration of it. After discussing the story, the children have an opportunity to comment on what they have read and seen and to ask questions. Ms. Crenshaw asks them to name the activities that took place in preparation for the Slava. Then she lists the activities on the board:

1. They killed the pig.
2. They painted the inside of the house.
3. They chopped wood, etc.

Next, she asks each child to select one activity from the list and to illustrate it. Four or five volunteers are given the job of making a bulletin board by grouping the completed pictures and suggesting a title for each group. The groups and their titles are presented to the whole class for

---

Information to be learned is related to pupils' experience.

---

discussion and modification. The class then decides on a single title for the completed bulletin board, e.g., "Preparing for the Slava." She concludes this lesson with a discussion about the preparations for festivals and holidays that are familiar to the children: Christmas, Passover, Thanksgiving, etc. As one basis for this discussion, she uses the categories in which the pictures are grouped.

The following day Ms. Crenshaw asks the pupils (in pairs) to recall and make lists of all the events that occurred during the Slava celebration as it was described in both the story and pictures. The class then pools its lists as follows:

1. The priest blessed the bread.
2. Food was carried upstairs.
3. The family story was told.
4. The children went to school, etc.

Pupils are asked to explain their reasoning processes.

Ms. Crenshaw now asks, "Which of these events take place every year in the same way?" As the children make suggestions, she asks them why they think so, and makes notes of their reasons. She then asks, "How do you suppose the people learned what to do at a Slava celebration?" When answers are not readily forthcoming, she suggests, "Think, for example, of the things *your* family does at Christmas, Passover, or Thanksgiving. How did your parents learn to do these things?"

The children respond: "They learned it from their parents"; "It was always done that way in the family"; etc.

She now writes the word "tradition" on the blackboard and asks them to help her formulate a definition of this word based on their previous

---

Pupils are encouraged to discover the concept rule.

---

discussions. Next she asks each of them to reconstruct all the events of their last family holiday—to list them, and then decide which events would and which ones would not satisfy their definition of "tradition."

Ms. Crenshaw plans to continue this unit on tradition by using the experiential examples provided by the children as a basis for further discussion and study of the following:

1. The variety of traditions represented by a group of children in a large city in the U.S. as compared to the similarity of traditions shared by villagers in Yugoslavia
2. Some similarities that exist even among differing traditions
3. The importance of tradition to *all* people.

Part 2: Procedures for Using the Concept Analysis Model in the Classroom

Teaching the idea of concepts to children is a three-step process. On the following pages are suggestions on how best to carry out the three steps indicated in Figure 11.

Figure 11. Steps in Using Concept Analysis

---

1. Select and examine the concepts to be taught.

2. Develop and use appropriate teaching strategies and related materials.

3. Develop and use appropriate assessment procedures.

---

1. Select and examine the concepts to be taught.

Locating the concepts. If the concepts important to your subject have not been identified in your curriculum guide or textbook and if you feel the need for direction, consult other courses of study or research-based curriculum development projects. Analyses have been done in such fields as science, math, and art, where efforts have been made to identify important concepts, to break them down into convenient subconcepts, and to specify the relationships among them.[9]

If you are planning a program for children in the early grades, you may wonder whether you really need such a detailed picture, particularly since you will be teaching only a few simple concepts. But, in fact, it will be useful for you to become aware of the entire structure of your subject area and the relationships among its more important concepts.

Making the selection. You will recall that a concept was defined as an idea (its name) and as having a rule (definition), attributes (characteristics which allow us to identify it), and references or exemplars (that to which the concept name may be applied). For the purposes of this model, it is important that you clearly identify and select the concepts that you wish to teach your pupils. Your choice(s) should be based on the importance and relevance of the concepts as well as on their usefulness within a particular subject area.

Here are some questions to guide your selection:

- Is the concept a prerequisite for other learning? (That is, will it have relevance to future learning in the same or other disciplines?)
- Is it needed by children to help them communicate with their peers? With adults? To help them understand the written materials? (That is, will it enable them to function more effectively in class?)
- Will it promote your pupils' problem-solving skills? (That is, will it be useful to them in the real world?)
- Will it help them develop self-esteem? (That is, will it help them define their own relationship to other people, places, things, and ideas?)
- Will it promote among them important societal goals? (That is, will it increase their potential contributions to society?)

The number of concepts you decide to teach will depend on their specificity. If you choose broad concepts that include many subconcepts, your list will probably be rather short. On the other hand, if you select concepts that are clearly defined and for which exemplars are readily available, your list may be somewhat longer. In either case, be sure to allow sufficient time to provide pupils with many opportunities for learning each concept.

Making sure you yourself understand the concepts. Preanalysis of a concept will ensure that you understand it, and also will help you plan both instructional and evaluative procedures.

Here are several guidelines [10] for analyzing a concept:

- Write down the concept's definition or rule.
- List its attributes, starring the critical ones (i.e., those that must always be present for the concept to exist).

• List, if possible, a sufficient number of exemplars and nonexemplars to incorporate into your instructional and evaluative materials.

• Identify any subconcepts contained within the attributes. (Remember that the subconcepts must be understood by pupils before they can learn the larger concept. If you subsequently discover your pupils have *not* mastered the subconcepts, you will obviously need to reteach them.)

Two examples of concept analyses are given in Figure 12.

Figure 12. Two Examples of Concept Analyses

Example 1

Name:
   "Slang"

Rule:
   An informal or nonstandard vocabulary that is used by a particular group within society and is likely to change or pass out of use quickly.

Attributes:
   1. Vocabulary—words or expressions
   2. Nonstandard
   3. Tied to a professional group, age group, regional group, or a group outside the mainstream of society
   4. Used to exclude nonmembers from a group
   5. Changes or passes out of use quickly (If the vocabulary persists and becomes widely used by many members of a society, it ceases to be called slang.)

Subconcepts that must be understood before new concept can be learned:
   1. Vocabulary—word, word combinations
   2. Nonstandard/standard distinctions
   3. Informal/formal distinctions
   4. Society
   5. Group
   6. Persistent usage

Exemplars:	*Nonexemplars:*
1. "pop a wheelie"	1. ride a bike with the front tire off the ground
2. "heavy"	2. serious, not frivolous
3. "hang loose"	3. stay calm, be relaxed

Figure 12 (continued)

Example 2

Name:
 "Food web"

Rule:
 The feeding (or eating) relationships among a community of living organisms that eat one another for the purpose of survival.

Attributes:
 1. A community—the habitat (common living area) and its inhabitants
 2. Organisms—living things, such as plants and animals
 3. Relationships—the dependency of one organism on another for the purpose of survival

Subconcepts that must be understood before new concept can be learned:
 1. Living/nonliving distinction
 2. Plant/animal distinction
 3. Survival
 4. Habitats
 5. Communities (groups of animals that live in the same area)

Exemplars:
1. Caterpillars eat leaves; birds eat caterpillars; etc.
2. Cows eat grass; people eat meat from cows.

Nonexemplars:
1. Birds drink water.
2. Calves get milk from their mothers.
3. People eat breakfast, lunch, dinner, etc.

Assessing the difficulty of a concept. The difficulty that you feel a concept will present to your pupils should determine how much time you will allot to the instruction of that concept. If the concept is likely to be a very difficult one, you should begin your instruction with a discussion of its subconcepts.

Figure 13 lists five criteria that you can use to help you determine the difficulty of any concept you may select:

1. Distance from child's experience.
2. Scope of concept (i.e., how many subconcepts it contains)
3. Ease with which exemplars can be identified or provided
4. Specificity of concept rule
5. Ways in which attributes of concept are related.

Figure 13. Assessing the Difficulty of a Concept[11]

Criteria (These criteria should be considered together, not separately.)	Scale of Difficulty		
	EASY ←		→ DIFFICULT
1. Distance from child's experience	Within direct experience	Within vicarious experience	Unrelated to past direct or vicarious experience
2. Scope of concept	Narrow scope; few concepts subsumed under it		Broad scope; many concepts subsumed under it
3. Ease with which exemplars can be identified or provided	Concrete referents; exemplars easily provided or identified		Highly abstract referents; exemplars difficult to provide or identify
4. Specificity of concept rule	Attributes clearly governed by law, rule, or scientific convention		Attributes dependent upon personal interpretation
5. Ways in which attributes of concept are related	Joint presence of several attributes	Presence of a set of attributes	Specified relationships among attributes

What follows is an example of how you might use Figure 13 to assess the difficulty of teaching the concept "slang" to children in the middle grades (as part of a larger unit on man and his language).

Criteria of Difficulty	*Scale of Difficulty*
1. Distance from child's experience (within his/her direct experience)	easy
2. Scope of concept	moderately difficult
3. Ease with which exemplars can be identified or provided	easy
4. Specificity of concept rule	moderately difficult
5. Ways in which attributes of concept are related	difficult

Slang is part of the direct experience of children, and children can be introduced to many varied exemplars. These facts should help to counterbalance the difficulty caused by two of the concept's attributes: the nonstandard nature of slang, and its mutability. (Incidentally, both of these attributes are themselves concepts that have to do with the relationship between man and his language.)

2. Develop and use appropriate teaching strategies and related materials.

A teaching strategy is simply a way of organizing or sequencing classroom procedures. In teaching concepts, it is useful to have several alternative strategies if possible. Research in the fields of child development and concept learning provides a number of useful ideas in this connection.[12] Some of these appear below.

Useful Ideas from Child Development Literature

1. *Elementary school children learn best through direct experience since their thinking processes are closely tied to their perceptions.*[13] When possible, bring concrete examples into the classroom. Recall Mr. Brown's science lesson. All his examples were tangible and manipulable. He asked children to classify objects by their material composition; he did not use pictures of objects or just the names of objects.

2. *The richer a child's environment (the sources from which the child selects and organizes his/her conceptual network), the more complete his/her concept development is likely to be.* Since there may be limits to the degree to which you can manipulate or enrich your classroom environment, you must sharpen the perceptions of the children to the point where they can make full use of whatever environment is available to them. For example, help

them develop the skill to observe and clearly describe what they see. Help them also to notice and talk about the world around them—the feel of it, the smell of it, the sound of it, the taste of it, the sight of it (color, shape, size). When you teach concepts having to do with human relationships, make the analogies to their own families, friends, acquaintances, and experiences.

3. *Do not expect children to be able to reason from abstractions or from hypothetical situations that are not directly related to their experience.* In this connection, recall Ms. Crenshaw's efforts to relate what the children were studying to their individual experiences.

4. *Children learn best by "discovering" a concept.* Provide your class with as many clearly distinguishable exemplars and nonexemplars as you can; then let the pupils define the distinctions between them. Recall Ms. Crenshaw's lesson and how the word "tradition" was not introduced until the children themselves had perceived several crucial dimensions of the concept.

5. *Children can have difficulty explaining their process of reasoning.* Children's often fumbling attempts to explain what they mean will help you understand their natural confusion. In fact, they themselves may be able to spot inconsistencies and internal contradictions.

Useful Ideas from Concept Learning Literature [14]

1. *In selecting your exemplars, be alert to extraneous or irrelevant material that may interfere with the student learning.* It is easier with certain concepts than with others to insert, delete, or manipulate aspects of exemplars. When direct manipulation is impossible, use verbal or written cues to differentiate between what is relevant to the concept and what is not. Recall that Mr. Brown supplemented the bars from the kit with other objects of differing sizes and shapes. He did this to ensure that the children would not simply focus on the size and shape of the bars in determining material composition.

2. *The sequence in which exemplars are introduced is also important.* The greater the apparent difference between an exemplar and a nonexemplar, the easier it will be for children to grasp the concept. Thus, begin with obvious contrasts before gradually moving to finer distinctions.

3. *If the concept lends itself to such treatment, provide clearly labeled exemplars and nonexemplars simultaneously.* The child can then more easily identify the attributes that distinguish exemplars from nonexemplars.

4. *The more varied the exemplars, the more opportunities children will have to identify relevant concept attributes and then generalize from them.* Recall how Ms. Crenshaw first asked her pupils to demonstrate their understanding of the concept by discriminating between exemplars and nonexemplars taken from their own experience, and then used their varied exemplars to emphasize the relevant attributes of the concept.

What follows is a summary of the foregoing suggestions:

- When possible, provide pupils with concrete examples that can be seen, touched, etc.
- Encourage them to explain their reasoning processes.
- Do not ask them to reason from abstractions or from hypothetical situations unrelated to their own experiences and perceptions.
- When possible, provide examples first and let pupils "discover" for themselves the concept rule.
- Help them develop skills of observation and description.
- When possible, manipulate exemplars in order to reduce or eliminate distractors (e.g., extraneous or irrelevant material that will interfere with the learning process).
- When possible, begin with exemplars and nonexemplars that are easy to differentiate and then move toward finer distinctions.
- Present as many exemplars and nonexemplars as time and suitability allow.
- When possible, present exemplars and nonexemplars *simultaneously*, so that pupils can more easily identify the crucial attributes that distinguish them from one another.

A Teaching Strategy for Concept Development

This teaching strategy, along with the following one for concept attainment, was developed by Hilda Taba and Associates as part of a social studies curriculum and is especially useful for a program based upon a concept analysis model. See Figure 14.

- Ask pupils to list or enumerate the attributes of a concept when given appropriate objects or information.
- Ask them to find several bases for grouping disparate items.
- Ask them to identify the common characteristics of grouped items, to label each group, and then to add new items to each group whenever feasible.
- Ask them to regroup and relabel items.[15]

Figure 14. Example of a Teaching Strategy for Concept Development [16]

Teacher	Student	Teacher Follow-Through
What do you see (notice, find) here?	Names items.	Makes sure items are visible or accessible to all students.
Do all of these items seem to belong together?	Suggests similarity as a basis for grouping items.	Demonstrates the grouping. For example: Underlines similarities in colored chalk, or marks them with symbols. Arranges objects, pictures, or cards.
Why would you group them together?*	Identifies and verbalizes the common characteristics of items in a group.	Seeks clarification of responses when necessary.
What would you call these groups you have formed?	Suggests a label (perhaps more than one word) that appropriately encompasses all items.	Records.
Could some of these belong in more than one group?	Offers other relationships.	Records.
Can we put these same items in different groups?† Why would you group them that way?	Offers other relationships.	Communicates grouping.

*Sometimes you may ask the same child "why" when he offers the grouping, and other times you may wish to get many groups before considering "why" things are grouped together.

†Although this step is important because it encourages flexibility, it will not be appropriate on all occasions.

Taba points out that it is crucial for children to do all the aforementioned operations for themselves. "The students," she says, "should see the relationships between items in their own way, figure out a basis on which to group items, and devise the categories or labels for the group." [17]

A Teaching Strategy for Concept Attainment [18]

See Figure 15.

• Ask children to say the concept word and then show the word in its printed form.

- Present children with a series of exemplars and nonexemplars.
- Ask children to distinguish exemplars from among a mixed group of exemplars and nonexemplars.
- Ask children to provide a definition of the concept.

3. Develop and use appropriate assessment procedures.

Assessing Young Children's Ability to Categorize

Young children vary in their ability to categorize objects and ideas. It is therefore important for you to know about each child's ability to

Figure 15. Example of a Teaching Strategy for Concept Attainment [19]

Teacher	Student	Teacher Follow-Through
"Say this word after me . . . ."	Repeats word.	Makes sure the word is pronounced correctly.
"This is an . . . ."	Looks at object; listens to description.	Checks for any who may not be able to see or hear.
"This is also an . . . ."	Gives, or reads statements which are illustrative examples of the concept.	
"This is not an . . . ."	Looks at new object, or listens to new description, or reads statements which are not examples of the concept (but which may be similar, in similar form, etc.).	Checks again.
"Show me an. . . ." or "Tell me what you think an . . . is." or "Which of these describes an . . . ?" or "Is this an . . . ?"	Points to object. Defines the concept. Selects from one or more descriptions.	Shows additional objects or gives fresh descriptions to test.
"How then would you define an . . . ?"	Gives summary generalization (definition) of concept.	Has students write down their definitions. Checks for accuracy.

categorize, no matter what the concept you are attempting to teach. You need such information to determine whether or not each child is able to learn the concepts in question.

According to Taba and Associates,[20] the reasons children give for placing an item in a particular group demonstrate that they use four different methods of grouping items:

1. *Mixed grouping.* The child will place an item in a group for one particular reason, and then will place yet another item in the group for a different reason. For example, given a collection of geometric shapes to sort, a child may begin by putting a blue triangle together with a red triangle (thus using triangularity as the basis for the grouping), and then add a red circle to the group (thus switching to redness as the basis for grouping).

2. *Functional or locational grouping.* A grouping may be made subjectively on the basis of a child's personal experience with the items. For example, when asked to provide a list of things generally found in a kitchen, he or she may list the following items: stove, refrigerator, sink, house slippers (because the mother keeps her house slippers in the kitchen), etc.

3. *Descriptive grouping.* Children may form groups because the items share a common characteristic: color, form, shape, texture, composition, etc. For example, they may group washing hair, watering plants, and boiling water for soup because all three activities involve water.

4. *Class groupings.* Groups are formed because of a characteristic or quality not observable in any one item, but which can be inferred from all of them. For example, activities such as cooking soup, peeling a carrot, and icing a cake would be grouped together because they all have to do with food preparation.

For purposes of concept development, children should be encouraged to progress from mixed or functional groupings to descriptive and class groupings. You should also remember that children sometimes have difficulty in seeing that an item can belong to more than one class (i.e., a man can be a father at the same time that he is a brother and a son). Children demonstrate flexibility when they are able to recognize that an item can be placed in more than one group, when they are able to regroup an assortment of objects or ideas, and when they can provide the item or group with a new label. The need to develop such flexibility is crucial to a child's understanding of relational concepts.

Figure 16. Assessing a Child's Flexibility Grouping[21]

Some Questions

---

1. How are these two things alike? How are they different?
2. Why did you put . . . with . . . ?
3. Could we put . . . with . . . ? Why or why not?
4. What things belong together? Why?
5. Can you put together all the things that belong together?
6. Why did you put them together?
7. Can you think of a word or a name to describe all these things (or ideas)?
8. Can you separate (or pick out) the . . . that are different (that don't belong)?
9. Why did you do it that way?
10. Now that you've arranged these in one way, is there any other way of arranging them?
11. Is there still another way these things could be put together?
12. Why did I put this item with that one? Would another one do as well? Why? Why not?
13. What makes these different?
14. What makes this go with that?
15. How are they related?
16. Are they related in still another way?

Figure 16 lists various types of questions you can use in assessing a child's method of grouping and his/her flexibility in grouping.

Figure 17 offers an example of how to keep a record of a pupil's progress in the area of grouping.

Figure 17. Sample Record of Pupils' Ability to Categorize[22]

Name	Date and Assignment	Mixed	Loca-tional	Descrip-tive	Class
John Jones	4/22 animal projects		✓		
	6/2 material objects			✓	
Mary Smith	4/22 animal projects	✓			
	6/2 material objects		✓		
Susan Brown	4/22 animal projects				✓
	6/2 material objects				✓

Assessing Children's Mastery of a Concept

One way to assess your pupils' mastery of a specific concept is to ask them to cite the rule, or describe the attributes of the concept. However, the most useful test of a child's attainment of a concept rests upon his or her ability to differentiate clearly between exemplars and nonexemplars.

Remember that the appropriate use of a concept label by a child does not necessarily prove that he or she has mastered the concept.

Figure 18 illustrates two types of check sheets that you can use to keep track of pupils' progress in concept attainment.

Part 3: Settings Needed When Using the Concept Analysis Model

Materials

Since children's concept development is based on their own experiences with concrete objects, you should find ways of providing them with materials other than textbook accounts, which are all too often "second-hand" experiences. Let your pupils use, manipulate, and work with these materials. Bring in "specimens" of the concept(s) under study. Conduct experiments. Take your class on field trips. Invite speakers to give demonstrations. Try to obtain films, tapes, etc., which will broaden your pupils' experiences with the concepts. And remember: The more exemplars you provide and the greater variety there is in your methods of presentation, the more likely it is your pupils will learn the concept.

It is important to use your pupils' responses to the materials as a measure of their value. If the pupils do not find them interesting or enjoyable (i.e., if they are not engaged by the materials), then the materials should be replaced. Materials that tend to capture the attention of young children are

- concrete and manipulable
- closely related to their interests (animals, sports, family relationships, etc.)
- game-like
- at an appropriate level of difficulty.

The pupils in your class will vary in their degree of conceptual development because of differences in their backgrounds and experiences. Thus, you will probably need to provide materials at various levels of difficulty. Efficient pupil assessment techniques (such as informal

Figure 18. Two Sample Check Sheets of Pupils' Concept Mastery

Example 1
Concept Mastery Sheet

Student Name	Mastery of Five Propaganda Techniques				
	name calling	bandwagon	glittering generalities	testimonal	plain folks
John	4/26	1/17			
Mary	2/3	1/18			
Sue	2/5	1/19			

(Continued)

Figure 18 (continued)

Example 2
Concept Mastery Sheet

Student Name: JOHN JONES	Mastery of Five Propaganda Techniques				
	name calling	bandwagon	glittering generalities	testimonial	plain folks
Able to name concept	4/21				
Able to use concept name appropriately	4/22				
Able to state concept rule	etc.				
Able to distinguish between relevant and irrelevant attributes					
Able to describe attributes clearly					
Able to distinguish between exemplars and nonexemplars					
Subconcepts that are causing problems:					
Additional comments:					

observations, conversations, and polls of the children as to their preferences) should help you make wise decisions in regard to choosing such materials.

As you begin to analyze the concepts you wish to teach, you will undoubtedly find that even the simplest of them possess unsuspected complexities which you must attend to if the concepts are to be presented to the children in clear, unmuddled fashion. Since no one person can be knowledgeable in every field, don't hesitate to seek help from curriculum guides or specialists in any of those areas where you do not feel comfortable.

Classroom organization

Many forms of classroom organization—ranging from whole-group to individualized instruction—can be used to help children learn concepts. Some pupils, for example, may need extra help in dealing with the subconcepts contained within the larger concept. In such an event, you may wish to provide them with self-correcting materials to help them move along at their own pace. Others may need practice in simple classification tasks so that they can move from mixed or locational groupings to descriptive or class groupings. In this case, you may have to set up special learning areas for them or choose special activities and materials.

On some occasions you may choose to introduce a concept to the entire class, while at other times you may want to have your pupils work in small groups. Sometimes children can learn a concept from their peers more easily than from an adult. You may wish to take advantage of this fact by training some of your pupils so that they can tutor younger members of the class or help those who are having difficulties with a particular concept. This system generally works to the benefit of both the children providing the instruction and those receiving it.

You may also find it necessary in certain cases to work with individual children as you seek to determine just what problems they are having with a specific concept and as you attempt to assess their mastery of the concept.

Personnel

Although you can, without help, guide and instruct your pupils through a program based on the concept analysis model, additional personnel can be useful—especially when you work with children individually. If you have aides in the classroom, be sure they have access to the concept analyses that you developed in the planning phase of the program.

Schedule

When the concept analysis model is used, it is not necessary to deviate from the normal classroom schedule unless you feel there is some good reason to do so.

Part 4: Anticipated Student Outcomes of Using the Concept Analysis Model

This section provides a list of skills that children may acquire from participating in a program based on the concept analysis model. The list is by no means exhaustive, so add to it and/or adapt it to the specific needs of your pupils.

The student outcomes listed below are written at two levels of specificity: Program objectives appearing in the left-hand column are general; related behaviors will be found in the right-hand column.*

Program Objectives	*Related Student Behaviors*

The pupil will select from the environment features or attributes that belong together.	1. Uses a consistent criterion for grouping
	2. Uses descriptive and class groupings rather than mixed and locational groupings
	3. Explains names or labels for groups
	4. Provides names or labels for groups
	5. Demonstrates flexibility in grouping
	  a. regroups, using consistent criteria
	  b. recognizes that one item can have simultaneous membership in more than one group.

The pupil will discover categories or concepts to understand and deal with the environment.	1. Identifies concept name 2. Uses concept name appropriately 3. States concept rule 4. Describes crucial concept attributes 5. Distinguishes between attributes that are crucial to the concept and those that are not.

*All outcomes should be rewritten in terms of your particular subject area.

Program Objectives	*Related Student Behaviors*
The pupil will recognize phenomena which do or do not exhibit specific features or attributes.	1. Differentiates between exemplars and nonexemplars 2. Provides other exemplars 3. Offers reasons for selecting appropriate exemplars while rejecting others.

Part 5: Checklists for Evaluating a Program Based on the Concept Analysis Model

The following two sets of checklists can be useful in evaluating the effectiveness of your program. The first checklist indicates how closely classroom procedures reflect the concept analysis model; the second checklist indicates whether or not your pupils are progressing according to your expectations.

Checklist 1

How closely do classroom procedures reflect the model?

	FREQUENTLY	SOMETIMES	SELDOM
• Pupils are provided with concrete examples of concepts that can be seen, touched, etc.	☐	☐	☐
• Pupils are provided with exemplars and then encouraged to "discover" the concept rules.	☐	☐	☐
• Pupils are provided with numerous different exemplars for a single concept.	☐	☐	☐
• When possible, pupils are provided with exemplars and nonexemplars simultaneously, so that they can more easily identify the crucial attributes that distinguish exemplars from nonexemplars.	☐	☐	☐
• Pupils are first presented with exemplars and nonexemplars that are easy to differentiate. Then they encounter those that require finer distinctions to be made.	☐	☐	☐
• The teacher presents exemplars in such a way as to reduce or eliminate distractors (extraneous or irrelevant material that is likely to interfere with the learning).	☐	☐	☐

Checklist 1 (continued)

	FREQUENTLY	SOMETIMES	SELDOM
• Pupils are encouraged to observe and describe.	☐	☐	☐
• Pupils are asked to explain their reasoning process.	☐	☐	☐
• Pupils are not asked to reason from abstractions or from hypothetical situations unrelated to their own experiences and perceptions.	☐	☐	☐

Are pupils given practice in:

	FREQUENTLY	SOMETIMES	SELDOM
• Grouping, labeling; regrouping, relabeling?	☐	☐	☐
• Naming concepts and using concept names appropriately?	☐	☐	☐
• Stating concept rules?	☐	☐	☐
• Distinguishing between relevant and irrelevant attributes?	☐	☐	☐
• Describing concept attributes?	☐	☐	☐
• Distinguishing between exemplars and nonexemplars?	☐	☐	☐
• Providing new exemplars of a concept?	☐	☐	☐

Checklist 2

Have pupils made progress in their ability and willingness to:

	YES	UNCERTAIN	NO		MOST STUDENTS	SOME STUDENTS	A FEW STUDENTS
• Group, label; regroup, relabel?	☐	☐	☐	or	☐	☐	☐
• Name concepts and use concept names appropriately?	☐	☐	☐		☐	☐	☐
• State concept rules?	☐	☐	☐		☐	☐	☐
• Distinguish between relevant and irrelevant attributes?	☐	☐	☐		☐	☐	☐
• Describe concept attributes?	☐	☐	☐		☐	☐	☐
• Distinguish between exemplars and nonexemplars?	☐	☐	☐		☐	☐	☐
• Provide new exemplars of a concept?	☐	☐	☐		☐	☐	☐

Part 6: References and Resources

Bruner, J. S., Goodnow, J., & Austin, G. *A Study of Thinking.* New York: Science Editions, 1962.

Durkin, M. C., & Tanabe, P. *Teacher's Guide for People in States.* Menlo Park, CA: Addison Wesley, 1973.

Joyce, B. R., & Weil, M. *Models of Teaching.* Englewood Cliffs, NJ: Prentice-Hall, 1972.

Joyce, B. R., Weil, M., & Wald, R. *Three Teaching Strategies for the Social Studies.* Chicago: Science Research Associates, 1974.

Lavatelli, C. S. *Piaget's Theory Applied to an Early Childhood Curriculum.* Boston: American Science and Engineering, 1970.

Martorella, P. H. *Concept Learning Designs for Instruction.* Scranton, PA: Intext Educational Publishers, 1972.

Nuffield Foundation. *I Do and I Understand; Beginning; The Duck Pond; Apparatus; Animals and Plants, and Others.* New York: John Wiley and Sons, 1967.

Piaget, J. *Judgement and Reasoning in the Child.* London: Routledge and Kegan Paul, 1928.

Science Curriculum Improvement Study. Boston: D. C. Heath and Company, 1967.

Taba, H., & Hills, J. L. *Teacher Handbook for Contra Costa Social Studies, Grades 1–6.* San Francisco: San Francisco College, 1967.

Taba, H., Levine, S., Freeman, F. E., & Elzey, F. *Thinking in Elementary School Children.* Cooperative Research Project No. 1574. San Francisco: San Francisco State College, 1964.

Appendix: Some Ideas from Jean Piaget on the Concept Development of Children[23]

Jean Piaget uses the word *egocentric* to describe the thinking processes of young children. He defines this to mean that their thinking is tied to their own viewpoint and not challenged by outside (contradictory) evidence.

In his view, young children's thinking processes differ qualitatively from the thinking processes of adults in several crucial ways:

1. Their reasoning is not constrained by logical necessity. They make judgments on the basis of individual instances, even though one judgment may directly contradict another.

> Grant (age 8) assigns the quality of being "alive" to fishes, "because they swim," to flowers, "because they grow," to the moon, "because it comes back in the evening," to the wind, "because it can blow," to fire, "because it burns," but he denies it to clouds, bicycles and watches, etc. "Water is not alive, it hasn't got any hands, it can't run on the grass."[24]

2. Although there is an underlying logic—albeit different from adult logic—which guides children's thinking, they have difficulty identifying or describing it to others.

> Im (age 6) subsumes three heterogenous notions [in his interpretation of the concept "alive"]—activity useful to man, the fact of giving heat (perhaps a variant of the first), and movement. In this way, clouds, sun, moon, stars, and wind are alive if considered from the angle of movement or activity (clouds are alive "because they show us the way") but are not alive if viewed from the angle of heat. For after telling us that the sun is alive "because it warms us" and the wind because it blows, Im says that fire is not alive "because it warms us and then it burns us" (non-useful activity), and neither is wind: "It blows, but it is not alive—Why?— because it makes us cold." Thus Im's three ideas of useful activity, heat and movement, clash. Wind is said to be alive when Im is thinking of its movement, and not alive when he is thinking of the cold which it causes. In this way, Im never succeeds in giving a fixed definition nor in becoming simultaneously conscious of the various factors which determine his thought at each moment of the interrogatory.[25]

3. Because young children often cannot identify or describe the logic they have used to arrive at a judgment, they cannot reason deductively. Similarly, since they are unaware of the rules they have used to reach conclusions, they are not disturbed by conclusions which may be contrary to rules.

4. Young children have difficulty grasping the relativity of such concepts as "friend," "enemy," "foreigner," etc. In describing the judgments of children, Piaget says they are "always absolute, so to speak, and never relative, for a relative judgment involves the simultaneous awareness of at least two personal points of view."[26] A concept as simple as "brother" is not understood by very young children, who use the word "brother" much as they would use the word "boy"—oblivious to the implied reciprocity: to have a brother, one must be a brother (or sister).

A dialogue with a four-year-old may go like this:

John, do you have a brother?	Yes
What is his name?	Jim
Does Jim have a brother?	No

5. Young children have difficulty in reasoning from a premise that conflicts with their own conceptions of reality. Thus, a child who was asked to solve an arithmetic problem involving five-headed dogs spent his time arguing that dogs have only one head.

6. Children tend to juxtapose propositions and classes rather than to establish their hierarchy. Piaget cites this example:

> The child is given . . . a test of this form: "If this animal has long ears it is a mule or a donkey; if it has a thick tail, it is a mule or a horse. Well, this animal has long ears and a thick tail. What is it?" . . . The child begins by considering the existence of long ears, and concludes that the animal must be a donkey or a mule. He then considers the existence of the thick tail. If this new condition were made to interfere with the preceding one, the child would eliminate the donkey since it has not got a thick tail. But the child considers this new condition separately, he juxtaposes it instead of contrasting it with the former condition, and he concludes that the animal may be a horse or a mule. . . . Finally . . . the child comes to the conclusion that all three cases [mule, donkey, horse] are possible. He therefore eliminates nothing.[27]

This tendency to juxtapose classes rather than establish hierarchies affects children's judgments about class inclusion and part-whole relationships. In questioning groups of children about their conceptions of "country," "city," "town," etc., Piaget discovered that to six- and seven-year-olds, "country" represented a unit alongside "town" and "district." Therefore, they would admit to being Genevans, but not Swiss. To children of eight and nine, towns and districts were seen as being in a country but not part of it—rather, surrounded by it. In fact, it wasn't until they were ten or eleven that these children saw themselves as being both Genevans and Swiss.

As children move through their elementary school years, they lay the foundation for adult patterns of logical thought. They begin to develop an awareness of the contradictions in their own thinking—contradictions which decrease as time goes on. They also begin to form classes in hierarchical order, to recognize relationships between and within classes, to differentiate their own point of view from the point of view of others, and to develop an awareness of their own thought processes. Finally, they develop flexibility of thought—i.e., they develop the ability to go back to the point at which they started to think about a problem and to compare it to their current thinking about that problem.

However, their thought processes are still closely tied to their perceptions and direct experiences. And it is not until the age of eleven or twelve that they are able to perform logical experiments that satisfy two conditions: "1) a 'mental experiment' carried out on the plane of pure possibility, and not as before on the plane of reality reproduced in thought; and 2) an ordering or awareness of the operations of thought as such, as for example of definitions or assumptions that one has made and has decided to retain identical with themselves."[28]

5
The Creative
Thinking Model

This model[1] provides a method for increasing the fluency, flexibility, and originality with which children approach objects, events, concepts, and feelings. It is based on the assumption that, in classroom situations where divergent responses are encouraged and respected, the students will benefit if they are taught specific techniques for thinking creatively.

Introduction

Creative thinking is often required for solving the problems of daily life as well as for composing a symphony or finding a cure for cancer. To function effectively in today's complex society, children must be taught to use their minds in creative ways.

What is creativity? Guilford and Hoepfner,[2] in their discussion of the creative process, make a distinction between two kinds of thinking: convergent and divergent. Convergent thinking is characterized by the search for a single conclusion or right answer. It is a process of marshaling and channeling information in pursuit of a solution that requires skills of memory, logic, and critical analysis. Divergent thinking, on the other hand, is a process less concerned with finding the single right answer and more concerned with exploring the many possible answers. It is characterized by fluency (the ability to generate many ideas), flexibility (the ability to entertain several ideas simultaneously), originality (the ability to generate ideas that are not commonplace), redefinition (the ability to see a situation or problem from alternative perspectives), and penetration (the ability to see beyond the obvious). Convergent thinking processes have long been emphasized in schools. Divergent thinking, which is more clearly associated with creative thinking, has traditionally received less attention there.

Although the study of creativity is still in its infancy, recent evidence seems to indicate that creative thinking skills can be developed through direct and systematic training and practice, and that the gap between an individual's creative talent and his creative output can be significantly narrowed by deliberate education in creative thinking techniques.

Several programs have been developed to teach creative thinking skills and to encourage in students a positive attitude toward creative ideas and activities. The creative thinking model attempts to synthesize and summarize some of these techniques as they are used in the following three programs:

- The Productive Thinking Program—Covington and Crutchfield[3]
- Lateral Thinking: Creativity Step by Step—E. DeBono[4]
- Synectics—W. J. J. Gordon[5]

Teaching children how to think creatively is a subject that raises many exciting issues and unanswered questions. It is recommended, therefore, that you spend some time reading and exploring the references as well as discovering others for yourself.

Assumptions of the creative thinking model

1. Fluency, flexibility, and originality are characteristics of creative thinking.
2. Creative thinking is a requisite for creative action.
3. Most children have the potential for increasing their creative output.
4. Creativity in thought and action does not occur spontaneously in classrooms in which assimilation of information is stressed.
5. Techniques for the development of creative thinking skills can and should be taught in school.

Part 1: Classroom Examples

Example 1

Ms. Fitzgerald took her third-grade class one day to see a display at the local art museum. After the children had been taken on the tour, Mr. Walsh, the art director, ushered them into a workroom. As he showed them a strange-looking object, he said: "This was part of a tool or a machine. I would like you to try to draw the whole machine or tool that this object was once part of."

He then passed out paper and crayons.

To Ms. Fitzgerald's disappointment, however, the children seemed to have a great deal of difficulty in doing the task. They continually asked whether they were "right." Many of them copied their tools or machines from a classmate; still others did not even begin.

Noting their difficulties, Mr. Walsh encouraged them by saying: "Don't be afraid to guess. Nobody knows what machine or tool this object was attached to. Try to think up your own imaginative machine."

But Ms. Fitzgerald was puzzled. Why did the children seem so afraid to use their imaginations? Were they concerned about what *she* might say? What the art director might say? Or were they simply intimidated by the museum setting? Whatever the reason, she decided she would try to teach them to be more creative and to enjoy thinking imaginatively.

Ms. Fitzgerald had already noticed that the children seemed to feel particularly relaxed and spontaneous during music activities. So one day, during a music lesson, she brought up the idea of machines again. She played different pieces of music and asked the children what machine the music made them think of. No one said anything. Ms. Fitzgerald then asked Johnny to come to the front of the room and to move in time to the rhythm. Johnny clapped his hands. One child said, "He's a clapping machine." Another child said, "He's either a tortilla maker or a pizza maker."

The class seemed to like very much the idea of the pizza-maker machine—so much so, in fact, that another child wanted to be a pizza-maker machine. He pretended to throw dough in the air in time to the music. Ms. Fitzgerald joined in by pretending to be a dough-stirring machine. The class then played a game of charades in which some of the children took turns portraying machines in time to different musical selections, while the others tried to guess what kind of machine was being portrayed.

The next day Ms. Fitzgerald played the "Just Suppose Game"[6] ("Just suppose there were a blueberry-picking machine, a paint-the-ceiling machine," etc.). Each child drew a "just suppose" machine. The drawings were then displayed and discussed, and Ms. Fitzgerald asked the children to think of what was especially interesting or unusual in each drawing.

After this, Ms. Fitzgerald introduced the "Association Game" in order to help the children look for analogies. Each child selected an animal and tried to relate this image to a machine ("An elephant is like a vacuum cleaner because . . ."). Later, the children stated a common problem (how to pick up trash without bending over, how to clean a narrow-necked bottle, how to find a lost softball, etc.) and tried to see whether anything that they knew of in the animal world sparked a new idea for solving the problem. Each child wrote down at least one analogy ("Finding a lost softball is like a dolphin finding food because . . ."). Ideas were explored and discussed, and, finally, each child evaluated his/her own ideas using a questionnaire previously prepared by Ms. Fitzgerald.

Example 2

Mr. Brown, a junior high school science teacher, uses analogies in class to make the strange familiar.[7] He talks, for example, about how cavities form, first describing the enamel and the slow process of decay through plaque formation and bacteria products, and then displaying a poster illustrating the various stages of tooth decay. After the pupils have listened to Mr. Brown's explanation, they ask questions and discuss what he has told them.

Mr. Brown then asks, "What can you think of that is like a tooth being eaten away?" Jim says that watering the yard is like a tooth being eaten away. Donna says that rust is like a cavity. In reply to Jim and Donna's suggestions, Mr. Brown goes on to ask, "How are watering the yard and rust like a cavity?" Jim says, "When you water the yard and leave the hose at one spot, the dirt gets eaten away." Donna says, "Rust forming on metal eats it away slowly."

Mr. Brown selects Donna's analogy as a means to explore the concept further. He says, "Donna, be a rusting metal can. How do you feel? What happens?"

Donna asks for time to do a little research on rust before she tries to answer the question. The next day, she describes the feeling of a rusting metal can as follows: "It's raining and raining! Oh, I don't like to be wet! I can feel drops of water on my skin. There are places on my skin that are beginning to hurt! Oh, look at the places on my skin that the rain has touched. They look funny. They're crumbling. There's no metal skin anymore—just ugly crumblies. I'm crumbling away—it's worse than disappearing!"

Mr. Brown asks the other pupils, "Can you describe some similarities and differences between rust and cavities?"

One pupil suggests that all metals rust, but not everyone gets cavities. Some of the pupils disagree with this statement. Janie volunteers to do some research on whether or not the statement is true. Donna suggests that bacteria are involved in cavities but not in rust. She thinks of this similarity: If you wipe away the water and make sure the metal is dry, you can prevent rust; and if you try to keep your teeth clean so that bacteria can't collect, you will have fewer cavities."

Mr. Brown then says, "We've had two analogies suggested and we've explored one of them. Can you think of any other things that are like cavities? How do they form? Write your ideas down. Then we'll share our ideas. Explain the reasons for your choice. Try to figure out similarities and differences."

The children think of the following analogies: Forming a cavity is like

- a woodpecker hammering at a tree
- ice melting
- forest fires starting
- a scab that forms when you fall down—only this time it doesn't heal
- a used tire.

Several children volunteer to share their ideas with the rest of the class. The analogies are then discussed and explored.

Mr. Brown *also* uses analogies to make the familiar strange. First he introduces the situation by stating that there must be an easier way to peel an egg. He says he gets annoyed when bits and pieces of the shell stick to the egg as he tries to remove the shell. Then he asks the class, "How could one peel an eggshell so that bits and pieces don't get left behind and you don't have to dig into the egg white to get them off?"

The pupils seem to be intrigued by this problem. Mark asks, "Does it have to be a person peeling an egg? Can it be a machine?"

Mr. Brown says a machine is acceptable *if* it can do the job. Then he solicits direct analogies by asking, "Can you think of an animal, plant, object, etc., that is easily peeled?"

Three suggestions are offered by the children—an onion, a flower, Scotch Tape.

Mr. Brown continues: "How are an onion, a flower, and Scotch Tape similar to an egg? Why did you choose these objects?"

Anna, who suggested the onion, says, "The onion has a thin brown skin we can't eat." Bobby, who suggested the flower, says, "The flower petals hide the inside of the flower, just as the eggshell hides the inside of the egg." "Scotch Tape has layers very close together, just like an eggshell," Cheri offers.

Mr. Brown decides to explore the Scotch Tape analogy first. He asks the children to make personal analogies. "Imagine you are the Scotch Tape," he says. "How would you feel when being peeled?"

Cheri replies, "I feel very close to my other layers. Each part of my insides is sticking right against the other layers. Someone is lifting me. Will part of me stick to the other layers and the other part be left off in a ragged mess? No! My body is somehow all stuck together, so all the pieces stay together."

Mr. Brown asks whether an onion would feel the same as Scotch Tape when it's being peeled.

Anna replies, "I'm an onion going to be peeled! I'm scared—human beings don't realize that if they peel onions wrong it hurts! There is a right way to peel me. I'm divided into layers with a special un-glue between each layer. The un-glue makes me separate easily. Wherever there is un-glue, I separate easily. Here comes a person who is going to peel me. Whew! Her fingernail finds the layer with the un-glue. That layer comes off very easily."

Mr. Brown then asks, "Now how can we make the eggshell act like Scotch Tape or an onion?"

One boy suggests that if the pieces of eggshell could stick together, the shell would not crack and come off in little bits. Another child says that if they could get some un-glue between the eggshell and egg, they could make the shell into onion sections that would come apart easily.

"Let's be practical," says Mr. Brown at this point. "Take your make-believe ideas and turn them into an actual eggshell peeler."

"I know," Raymond says. "We could paint a sticky glue on the eggshell so pieces would stick together and come off easier. Once we got a little bit off, the rest of the pieces of eggshell would lift off without our having to fool with it much."

Cheri has another idea. "Make a hole in the eggshell," she exclaims, "and force air in it so there is a layer of air between the shell and the egg—like a layer of un-glue. Then there would be better separation—just like an onion section."

Part 2: Procedures for Using the Creative Thinking Model in the Classroom

Creative thinking can effectively be taught by using the three steps shown in Figure 19. Each step is discussed in some detail in the following pages.

Figure 19. Steps in Using Creative Thinking

---

1. Establish a climate that fosters creative thinking.

2. Teach pupils to use techniques that lead to creative ideas and products.

3. Evaluate and test the ideas that have been offered.

---

1. Establish a climate that fosters creative thinking.

Creative thinking flourishes best in a stimulating, challenging atmosphere where children are not fearful of being wrong and where new and unusual ideas are offered and tried out. In such an atmosphere, the hard thinking needed to create new ideas and to solve problems imaginatively is likely to be a pleasurable experience.

You, the teacher, must try to create such an atmosphere. To do this, you must genuinely believe that creative thinking skills are very important for children to acquire. You must convey this belief to your pupils and teach them to value both the processes and the products of creative thinking. You must also make sure that *all* ideas are welcomed, not only for their immediate usefulness, but for their ingenuity and for their value in leading the class to new ideas and directions. Remember: Ideas should never be belittled, no matter how outlandish they may seem at first.

Here are some ways to create a climate that will foster among your students the development of creative thinking skills.[8]

1. *Allow the class time to think.* Innovation and creativity rarely occur when there is too much time pressure. Many creative ideas come about

only after an "incubation" or rest period when the problem is not being actively worked on. So resist the temptation to rush your students or to tell them which is the best way to find a solution to a problem. This practice may *seem* to save time, but in the long run it will stifle initiative and inhibit the innovative ideas and solutions your pupils might otherwise have offered. Overemphasizing "correctness" will similarly inhibit creativity.

2. *Discuss with the class the value of unusual ideas.* Introduce them to the notion that unusual ideas have frequently resulted in useful inventions. For example, there are many machines that were considered "crazy" at the time they were first presented—the Wright brothers' "flying machine," Ford's "horseless carriage," etc. Stress the fact that many creative people go against the popular ideas of their time. Then discuss the need for unusual ideas in many phases of life—technology, the arts, science, literature, etc. You may also wish to retrace the steps through which great ideas were conceived and developed.

3. *Become aware of your children's creative activities in all areas of their lives and help them to recognize the ways in which they act creatively.* Even though you may be their teacher in only one subject area, make an effort to know about their other interests so that you can express your approval of their creative endeavors and thereby encourage them to value their own creativity.

4. *Help them become aware of the deficiencies and discrepancies in many commonly accepted explanations and beliefs.* Find opportunities to play the "devil's advocate," and challenge the assumptions they commonly hold (e.g., the sky is blue).

5. *Make sure there is no testlike atmosphere surrounding the creative activities you introduce them to.* Their ideas, of course, will be evaluated, but "right" and "wrong" should not be the way to judge their creative efforts.

6. *Help your students to see that there is value in another person's ideas.* Peer pressure can often squelch creativity. The children in your program should learn to become tolerant of ideas that may seem "crazy" to them or different from those that are commonly offered and accepted by the peer culture. If a child offers an unusual idea that is not valued by the rest of the class, work with that child and help him/her to refine it. Explain to the other children what you are doing, and why. In short, don't let unusual ideas get lost for lack of attention.

7. *Help your pupils to become more open and sensitive to their environment.* Work hard at making them good observers. Encourage them to notice details. For example, after showing them a picture of an unusual or ambiguous situation, ask them to explain the picture and to support their

interpretation by identifying details in the picture which led them to their interpretation.

8. *Encourage them to participate in activities that give them practice in fluent thinking.* A few examples of such activities might be:

- Make up several titles for a story, each of which stresses a different aspect of the story.
- Make up many different stories as a way of explaining a picture or part of a picture.
- Offer several uses for a common object (e.g., a pencil can be used to write, to plug holes, to poke holes, to shape dough or clay, as a rhythm instrument, etc.).
- Use a single set of geometric shapes in such a way as to make many different designs. (See the examples below.)
- Describe a geometric object in a variety of ways. (See examples.)

Geometric Designs

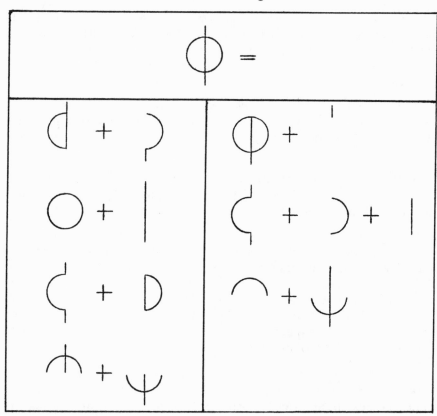

2. Teach pupils to use techniques that lead to creative ideas and products.[9]

Although there are a variety of techniques that can be used to stimulate creative thinking, they all work best when

- pupils are in an "accepting" environment—one that both allows and stimulates them to give several responses to the same question, problem, or situation
- the teacher sees his/her role as that of providing cues and procedures to help pupils create their own ideas, rather than that of dispensing information and "right" answers
- situations are created for which conventional responses either are not available or will not be effective.

Techniques that lead to the production of creative ideas can be applied to most subject areas, problems, or situations. As you present and apply these techniques, be sure to name and explain each one to the children and to use as many examples as possible. Knowing the names or labels will help your pupils to recall, use, combine, and adapt the techniques.

The labels provided below were chosen because of their frequent use in current research. Since many of them are difficult, some additional "children's labels" have been provided. However, feel free to invent your own. In either event, it is important to remember that the procedures you will find listed under each technique or group of techniques should serve only as guides, *not* as rigid "rules." BE CREATIVE; adapt and combine them or develop others.

Some Creative Thinking Techniques [10]

For each of the following techniques, there is a short list of procedures which indicates how you might use it with the pupils in your class. As you will see, although the techniques have different labels, they have some important characteristics in common. You will also find some more suitable or comfortable to use than others. Note, too, that in the Appendix of this model, each of these techniques is described in greater detail.

Technique 1: Focusing on unnoticed characteristics, objects, or relationships

1. Present the children with a situation or a problem.
2. Elicit their observations about the situation or their solutions to the problem.
3. List those characteristics, objects, or relationships which the children seem to be attending to.

4. Together with the children, examine the situation or problem to find other, less apparent characteristics, objects, or relationships.
5. Choose one of these neglected details, and explore the new solutions which might result.

Technique 2: Challenging your own assumptions (Don't take anything for granted.)

1. Present the children with a common, widely held assumption, e.g., "Smart kids get good grades."
2. Ask the children to analyze this assumption by
   • turning it around to see if it still applies (e.g., "Good grades mean you're smart.")
   • adding modifiers to find the limits of the assumption (e.g., "*All* smart kids get good grades.")
   • changing parts of the statement and exploring the implications (e.g., "Smart kids get *bad* grades.").
3. Ask the children how they would "check out" (empirically verify) the assumption, and provide them with the necessary guidance to do this.

Technique 3: Constructing an idea tree

1. Present the class with a problem situation.
2. Elicit three or four general categories for exploration.
3. Construct an idea tree using these categories as the large limbs of the tree.
4. With the class's help, provide the tree with appropriate branches—i.e., specific ideas.
5. Provide the class with a new, but comparable problem situation and ask them to construct their own idea tree.

Technique 4: Changing the dominant set

1. Present the class with a problem situation.
2. Elicit ideas and suggestions for solutions.
3. List the suggestions on the board; then ask the children to group them and to label each group.
4. Ask for suggestions that do *not* fit in with the existing labels.
5. If the children find this hard to do, provide them with new labels or groups as a way to stimulate further exploration.

Technique 5: Looking for puzzling facts or events

1. Encourage the class to view every situation as a potential source of interesting problems, questions, or conundrums.

2. Ask them to bring to class examples of ambiguities and discrepancies from their own experience.
3. Elicit varied explanations for a given event. (To do this, you might want to use some of the preceding techniques.)
4. Provide the pupils with situations for which there is no single explanation, and encourage them to be comfortable with more than one possible explanation.
5. Provide historical examples of how mistakes or accidents were used as an impetus for new directions of thought.
6. Use pupils' "errors" as starting points for changing their perspectives and exploring new ideas.

Technique 6: Exploring your thinking through subtraction and reversal

1. Present a problem situation.
2. Elicit suggestions for solutions by asking the pupils to
   • subtract a quantity or characteristic from an entity within the problem situation
   • remove the need for an entity within the problem situation
   • proceed in an opposite direction when attempting to arrive at a given point within the problem situation
   • reverse a relationship within the problem situation.
3. Present other problem situations and encourage pupils to select a method for reversing their thinking and then applying it to each situation.

Technique 7: Putting yourself in another person's shoes

1. Present a problem situation (e.g., "Imagine that you are this person . . .").
2. Ask pupils to describe the problem from the point of view of the other person (e.g. "My problem is . . .").
3. Ask pupils to act out the problem in pantomime (if the problem is amenable to such a procedure).
4. Discuss the various suggestions and ideas that emerge from the above procedures.

or

1a. Present an interpersonal situation or problem.
2a. Ask for suggestions for resolving the problem, and list the ideas that emerge.
3a. Ask the children to role play[11] the various ideas that are suggested.

4a. Explore the feelings and attitudes that emerge from the role-playing activities.

Technique 8: Working backwards ("Just suppose")

1. Present the class with a point of view, a problem and its solution, or a hypothetical situation.
2. Ask the pupils to
   • develop arguments in defense of the point of view, or else to
   • work backwards, tracing the steps from the solution to the problem as they do so
   • develop a methodology for changing a hypothetical situation into a real situation.
3. Discuss and evaluate student responses by examining
   • the efficacy of the arguments
   • the logic and comprehensiveness of the steps leading from the solution to the problem
   • the potential and originality of the methodology.

Technique 9: Making predictions and considering consequences ("Guess what's going to happen")

1. Present the class with a situation—hypothetical or real.
2. Ask the pupils to make predictions about what will happen.
3. Discuss each prediction in terms of its relationship to the situation.
4. Ask the children to consider how their predictions would be different if one element in the situation were to be changed.
5. Encourage the pupils to present situations of their own for class consideration.

Technique 10: Using analogies to make the strange familiar [12]

1. Provide information on a topic or subject that is new to the children.
2. Ask them for direct analogies (e.g., "What object, idea, feeling, event that we know is like this?" "How are _____ and _____ alike?") Try to select objects that are as unrelated as possible, since these tend to make children "stretch" for the comparisons.
3. Ask them to empathize with an entity in their analogy ("Be the thing."). Ask them too, "What does it feel like?" "Where are you?" "What are others doing to you?"
4. Re-explore the above relationships in light of the insights gained from the "be the thing" experiences.
5. Elicit other analogies for the unfamiliar topic; then explore these connections in the same manner.

Technique 11: Using analogies to make the familiar strange

1. Elicit or present a problem or situation known to the pupils and then discuss it.
2. Ask the pupils to think of other objects, ideas, or events which may have similarities with this subject or the problem.
3. Explore and describe the connections between the analogous entities.
4. Ask the pupils to empathize with an entity in their analogy ("Be the thing.").
5. In light of the insights they gained from the "be the thing" experiences, ask them to see the familiar in a new way.

3. Evaluate and test the ideas that have been offered.

Children need other people to react to their creative ideas, not only because this feedback satisfies their curiosity about how "the world" sees their ideas, but also because it helps to guide them in subsequent creative endeavors. This being the case, provide the students with numerous opportunities to test and evaluate their own, as well as each other's, ideas and products.

Say, for example, that you present students with a problem and ask them to "brainstorm" and thus generate ideas that might lead to a solution. The "rules" of brainstorming require that each individual be allowed to suggest anything that comes to mind and that no one will inhibit this free flow of ideas by commenting on the value or worth of any idea. All ideas are then written down. When the brainstorming session no longer produces anything meaningful, the ideas can then be evaluated by categorizing them.

Here are a few suggested ways of doing this:

- *"We'll try this."* (Ideas that seem obviously useful.)
- *"Interesting, but not practical."* (Ideas that introduce a novel perspective but do not readily lend themselves to practical application. All new perspectives should be acknowledged and encouraged, regardless of the practicability of the resulting suggestions.)
- *"Part of the idea is useful."* (Ideas that are not totally useful but that contain a useful element.)
- *"We need more information on these ideas."* (Ideas that stimulate or direct a search for more information.)
- *"It's been tried already. Let's investigate and see how well the idea has worked."* (Ideas that represent existing practices.)

Once the pupils have categorized their ideas, they can go on to a consideration of their consequences. In some situations, they can even make arrangements to try out the most promising ideas.

Care must be taken so that any evaluation activities that you introduce do not inhibit spontaneity. The atmosphere must not become threatening or critical. As the children discuss or comment on their own work or that of others, you should stress that they are helping and learning from one another.

Often, it is good to let some time elapse between the production of ideas and their evaluation. This helps the children to view their ideas and creations more objectively and will make the evaluation a less intrusive and inhibiting experience for all.

Part 3: Settings Needed When Using the Creative Thinking Model

Materials

Some materials are designed specifically to stimulate creative thinking. Since they usually contain puzzlements, oddities, obvious discrepancies, and mysteries, they will probably stimulate multiple and unusual responses. In short, there will be no single "right" answer to the situations they present.

You can also use traditional materials to teach creative thinking using the following techniques as guides:

• Rather than asking the children to discuss or analyze a story they have read, ask them instead to retell the story from the point of view of one of the minor characters.

• Rather than presenting the children with computation tasks, design a code system that requires computation in order for them to decode the secret message.

• Instead of simply dismissing a child's erroneous answer in a social studies class, develop an entire lesson based on how history might have turned out differently had the mistaken answer been correct.

Classroom organization

Different activities call for different classroom organizations. However, there is no special way to organize your classroom when using this model. Some creative thinking activities may call for either large or small group instruction; others for individual work.

Personnel

Whether or not you need additional help will depend upon the activities you plan for your class. If you wish to divide the pupils into small groups, or if you have a few children who tend to be distracting elements, it might be a good idea to enlist a teacher's aide or some other helper. If you do, it is important to make sure that these adult helpers are familiar with the attitudes, techniques, and environment necessary for teaching creative thinking.

Schedule

The teaching of creative thinking can be scheduled quite flexibly. For example, in one activity the children may need a certain amount of time for generating ideas, and more (or less) time for discussion and evaluation. But whatever schedule you employ, it should reflect the special needs of *your* children. Answering some of the following questions may help you plan your schedule:

- Is the climate of my classroom conducive to free and imaginative thinking? If not, how long will it take me to establish the proper climate?
- How much previous experience do my pupils have in creative thinking?
- How much background do they have in the subject areas I wish to cover?
- Can they reach satisfactory solutions and/or generate a sufficient number of ideas in one session? If not, how many sessions will be necessary?
- Should I apply my creative thinking techniques within existing subject areas, or will they cover material outside those areas?

You will find a sample schedule for a teacher's creative thinking activities in Figure 20 on the next page.

Part 4: Anticipated Student Outcomes of Using the Creative Thinking Model

This section provides a list of skills that children may acquire from participating in a program based on the creative thinking model. The list is by no means exhaustive, so add to it and/or adapt it to the specific needs of your pupils.

Figure 20. A Sample Five-Week Schedule

Schedule

Week 1
• Review musical concepts (rhythm, harmony, melody line, dynamics, etc.).
• Review musical instrument "families" (show film).

Week 2
• Listen to examples of "natural music" (sounds from nature).
• Discuss the "music" of whale sounds, bird songs, other animal noises, wind sounds, water sounds, etc.
• Have students, working in groups, bring to class examples of "music" made by machines (homework assignment).

Week 3
• Play American and European folk music for class.
• Discuss elements basic to folk music.
• Focus on one or two elements in a given piece of music and "play" with it or them.
• Change an element to see what happens to the music.
• "Create" a folk song b*y* having children work in groups.

Week 4
• Play African, South American, and Asian folk music.
• Discuss typical instruments used in this music.
• Have students make an instrument out of a common household object (homework).
• "Orchestrate" a folk song with students playing their homemade instruments.

Week 5
• Use analogy techniques to explore with class the relationship between people and music, by asking such questions as
  —How is listening to music like eating?
  —How is music like speech? Like war? Like peace?
• Elicit further analogies from the students.
• Have students write an essay critiquing unit (homework; essays to be read in class).

The student outcomes listed below are written at two levels of specificity: Program objectives appearing in the left-hand column are general; related behaviors will be found in the right-and column.*

Program Objectives	*Related Student Behaviors*
The pupil will develop attitudes conducive to creative thinking.	1. Exhibits interest in range of subject areas
	2. Works at a problem when the correct answer is uncertain or perhaps unavailable
	3. Asks questions about the "commonplace" things around him/her
	4. Identifies unusual ideas
	5. Generates alternative ideas without asking whether they are "right" or whether he/she is "getting close" to the answer
	6. Tries to arrive at the answer to a problem on his/her own
	7. Defends an idea even if it differs from the majority opinion
	8. Seeks to find ways to use his/her mistakes
	9. Changes or modifies his/her opinion when confronted with new information
	10. Listens to ideas and explanations of others without interrupting.
The pupil will be able to test and evaluate ideas or suggestions objectively.	1. Given a problem and a list of ideas for solution, can select ideas which are directly related to solving the problem
	2. Given a list of ideas that are seemingly not useful, can extract whatever may be useful
	3. Can identify ideas which offer new approaches to a problem
	4. Can devise tests to try out new ideas
	5. Can imagine consequences for proposed ideas
	6. Seeks ways to refine or improve an idea.

*All outcomes should be rewritten in terms of your particular subject area.

Program Objectives	*Related Student Behaviors*
The pupil will be able to use problem reformulation as a way of generating new ideas and products.	1. Can attend to various characteristics of an object, or to various objects in a given situation 2. Can name more than one relationship in a situation 3. Can question commonly held explanations and beliefs 4. When solving problems or generating ideas, can think of a general statement from which more specific ideas may arise 5. Can classify ideas according to various characteristics 6. Can produce a modification by "taking away" a quality or part of an object, or a portion of a given situation 7. Given a relationship, can change the "acted upon" to the "actor" in order to arrive at new ideas about the situation 8. Can identify opposing sides of a problem or situation 9. Can change the way in which he/she perceives a problem.
The pupil will be able to recognize puzzlements and discrepancies and use them to generate new ideas.	1. Can "tease out" unrecognized discrepancies or errors in ideas that are normally taken for granted 2. Can formulate "new" explanations for such ambiguous events 3. Tries out a variety of explanations to see which best explains a seeming discrepancy 4. Can think of an explanation that accounts for a number of puzzling events or discrepancies.
The pupil will be able to use analogies as a means of generating new ideas.	1. Can use analogies to generate a "new look" at familiar things 2. Can use analogies to relate the unfamiliar to more familiar objects 3. Given a particular object, can name another object that is related in some way

Program Objectives	*Related Student Behaviors*
(analogies, *continued*)	4. Can use environment as a source for discovering relationships between things
	5. Can name the similarities and differences between two objects
	6. Can change his/her viewpoint by taking the view of another person, an animal, or a thing.

Part 5: Checklists for Evaluating a Program Based on the Creative Thinking Model

The following two sets of checklists can be useful in evaluating the effectiveness of your program. The first checklist indicates how closely classroom procedures reflect the creative thinking model; the second checklist indicates whether or not your pupils are progressing according to your expectations.

Checklist 1

How closely do classroom procedures reflect the model?

	FREQUENTLY	SOMETIMES	SELDOM
• Pupils are encouraged to value "unusual" ideas.	☐	☐	☐
• Teacher refrains from telling pupils what is "best" or "right."	☐	☐	☐
• Activities are conducted in a "test-free" atmosphere.	☐	☐	☐
• Pupils are rewarded for creative efforts and unusual ideas.	☐	☐	☐
• Pupils' ideas are never belittled, no matter how outlandish they seem.	☐	☐	☐
• Pupils are provided with sufficient time to think about an idea before they are asked to respond to it.	☐	☐	☐
• Teacher introduces creative thinking techniques, naming and explaining them as he or she does so.	☐	☐	☐
• Pupils are provided with ample opportunities to present their work to the class.	☐	☐	☐

Checklist 1 (continued)

Are pupils given practice in:

	FREQUENTLY	SOMETIMES	SELDOM
• Identifying and using a variety of creative techniques?	☐	☐	☐
• Reformulating problem situations?	☐	☐	☐
• Recognizing situations containing puzzlements and oddities?	☐	☐	☐
• Using analogies to generate new ideas?	☐	☐	☐
• Selecting useful problem-solving ideas from a pool of ideas?	☐	☐	☐
• Extracting whatever part of an idea is useful?	☐	☐	☐
• Imagining consequences for proposed ideas?	☐	☐	☐
• Devising tests to try out ideas?	☐	☐	☐
• Identifying ideas that offer new perspectives?	☐	☐	☐

Checklist 2

Have pupils made progress in their ability and willingness to:

	YES	UNCERTAIN	NO	or	MOST STUDENTS	SOME STUDENTS	A FEW STUDENTS
• Identify and use a variety of creative techniques?	☐	☐	☐	or	☐	☐	☐
• Reformulate problem situations?	☐	☐	☐		☐	☐	☐
• Recognize situations containing puzzlements and oddities?	☐	☐	☐		☐	☐	☐
• Use analogies to generate new ideas?	☐	☐	☐		☐	☐	☐
• Select useful problem-solving ideas from a pool of ideas?	☐	☐	☐		☐	☐	☐
• Extract whatever part of an idea is useful?	☐	☐	☐		☐	☐	☐
• Devise tests to try out new ideas?	☐	☐	☐		☐	☐	☐
• Identify ideas that offer new perspectives?	☐	☐	☐		☐	☐	☐

Part 6: References and Resources

Covington, M., Crutchfield, R., Davies, L., & Olton, R. *The Productive Thinking Program.* Columbus, OH: Charles E. Merrill, 1972.

Davis, G. A., & Scott, J. A. *Training Creative Thinking.* New York: Holt, Rinehart, and Winston, 1971.

DeBono, E. *Lateral Thinking: Creativity Step by Step.* New York: Harper and Row, 1970.

Gordon, W. J. J. *The Metaphorical Way of Learning and Knowing.* Cambridge, MA: Porpoise Books, 1971.

Guilford, J. P. "Traits of Creativity." In H. H. Anderson (Ed.), *Creativity and Its Cultivation: Interdisciplinary Symposium on Creativity.* New York: Harper and Row, 1959.

Guilford, J. P., & Hoepfner, R. *The Analysis of Intelligence.* New York: McGraw-Hill, 1971.

Joyce, B. R., & Weil, M. *Models of Teaching.* Englewood Cliffs, NJ: Prentice-Hall, 1972.

Taylor, C. W. (Ed.). *Creativity: Progress and Potential.* New York: McGraw-Hill, 1964.

Wallach, M. A., & Kogan, N. *Modes of Thinking in Young Children.* New York: Holt, Rinehart, and Winston, 1965.

Appendix

This section contains descriptions and examples of eleven techniques for encouraging creative thinking:

1. Focus on unnoticed characteristics, objects, or relationships.
2. Challenge your assumptions.
3. Construct an idea tree.
4. Change the dominant set.
5. Look for puzzling facts or events.
6. Explore your thinking through subtraction and reversal.
7. Put yourself in another person's shoes.
8. Work backwards.
9. Make predictions and consider consequences.
10. Use analogies to make the strange familiar.
11. Use analogies to make the familiar strange.

1. Focus on unnoticed characteristics, objects, or relationships.

Encouraging your pupils to focus on characteristics which they do not usually attend to is one way of helping them produce imaginative, insightful responses. For example, suppose you ask your class to write an essay or poem about a tree. Many children would focus on the general appearance of a tree—its height, the number of its branches, the spread of the branches, etc. What would happen, though, if you were to ask the children to focus on and write about a *single* characteristic of the tree—the way it smelled, sounded, or felt—or about the suggestive shape of one of its leaves or branches?

Looking at a single, often overlooked object in a situation can also help reset your pupils' focus. Having them read an exciting poem or essay about a tree may result in their looking closely at a single gnarled burl on the tree or examining one of the beetles that live in the tree.

Another way to change student focus is to introduce to them the idea of spatial or structural relationships. For example, if you are having a lesson on the human body, an unusual object of study might be the relationship between the joint system and body movement. In this connection, consider the creative possibilities of an assignment that asks pupils to design a joint system which would enable someone to do things he/she cannot presently do (e.g., turn one's head around completely, coil up like a snake, etc.).

Solving problems creatively requires that one look for characteristics, objects, or relationships that are often overlooked. Here's an example:

You go with two friends to a restaurant. After dinner, one of them gets sicks. Neither you nor your other friend feels any sickness or discomfort—but, then you all ordered different things. When the doctor arrives, he asks if you can think of any likely causes of your unfortunate friend's illness.

If it is determined that the food he ate was not spoiled, you might then *focus on unnoticed characteristics.* For example, do you remember how much of the food your friend ate? Or the spices used in the food?

You might also inquire about the state of your friend's health. Was he well that night? Did he have any disease?

The next thing you might do is to *focus on unnoticed objects.* You decide now to look at the plates on which the food was served. Were they clean? How conscientiously do the restaurant's waiters, cooks, and busboys observe sanitation rules?

What other objects might you have noticed—a person who was dining nearby, the restrooms, an object outside the restaurant, other living objects in the restaurant? Could your friend possibly have been bitten by an insect?

Your third step might be to *focus on unnoticed relationships.* You might look, for example, at the time relationship: What was your friend doing immediately prior to the onset of his symptoms? What other relationships went unnoticed at the time? What about spatial relationships? Where was he when he got sick? Who else was there?

2. Challenge your own assumptions.

All of us operate out of a great many assumptions which we may or may not realize we hold. Sometimes we can make our assumptions explicit and thus can easily examine them. Sometimes, though, our assumptions are implicit, and so we take them for granted. But doing this may impede our problem-solving or productive thinking abilities. For example, some people have trouble learning another language because they assume, without being aware of it, that the second language is based on a grammatical structure identical to that of their native language.

Problems

What follows are some problems which will help reveal some of your own assumptions that you may not be aware of.[13] (The answers are below.)

a. *The nine-dot puzzle.* Connect the nine dots below using only four straight lines. You may go in any direction, but once you have started, you may not raise your pencil from the paper.

●   ●   ●

●   ●   ●

●   ●   ●

b. *How good a marksman are you?* Darken the center of each flower with your pencil—while your eyes are closed.

c. *The pear brandy mystery.* Inside a bottle of pear brandy there is a whole pear. How did the pear get into the bottle? What is your guess?

Solutions

Problem a.

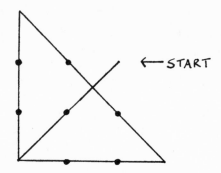

Did you assume that your lines could *not* go beyond the square outline formed by the dots? But there were no directions to that effect. An implicit assumption!

Problem b. Make a "bump" in the center of each flower with your pencil. Then, with your eyes closed, feel for the bumps and mark them with your pencil.

Did you assume that such a plan would be cheating? If so, on what do you base this assumption? No rules were set forth for doing this task. Another implicit assumption!

Problem c. Did you assume that the pear was fully grown before it was placed in the bottle? What made you assume that? If a bottle were placed on a tree over a branch bearing a pear bud, the solution is simple. Your failure to find it was due to—yes, still another implicit assumption!

3. Construct an idea tree.[14]

When trying to figure something out, people often follow only a single train of thought. For example, when asked to think of things that float, they tend to picture a body of water and then try to imagine what might be floating on it.

Rather than using just one image as the springboard for ideas, it can be helpful to think of several possibilities. For example, you might picture not only a body of water, but a sky, an eye, maybe outer space even. These general possibilities can help you to generate many specific ideas.

Using an idea tree is a good way to ensure that alternative lines of thought are not overlooked and that the search for ideas is as complete as possible. It not only keeps you from getting "stuck" with one perspective, but helps you plot out many perspectives or sets before you start thinking of specific ideas.

This technique can be represented graphically by using a tree whose big limbs contain the broad, general possibilities, whereas the smaller branches contain the particular ideas suggested by each main or general idea.

For example, say that you want to investigate the reasons for continued conflict between two countries. The "idea tree" will help you explore these reasons from a number of different perspectives. (See the tree on the next page.)

4. Change the dominant set.[15]

Thinking can become more productive when the perspective from which one is working is first identified and then changed. Identifying your perspective requires that you examine your ideas, categorize them, and then label them. The label helps you identify your perspective or set. Once this has been identified, you can change sets by thinking of other themes to pursue.

You probably have had the experience of asking a number of pupils to offer an original suggestion only to get variations on the same theme that was established by the child who spoke first. Using the technique of changing the dominant set, you would list all suggestions on the blackboard, help the children identify the set that is heavily influencing their ideas, and then help them to change their perspective by asking for, or suggesting, ideas of another type. (Most young children will almost certainly need your help in doing this.)

Here is an example of how this technique works.

Let's say you have asked your class: How can you show that the air is everywhere? These are some of the responses you get:

• The windmill turns because the wind (air) pushes against it.
• Trees move with the wind.
• A fan pushes air. You can feel the air as the fan whirls around.
• If you turn the leaves of a book quickly, you can make a small wind.

Although all these statements are correct, they are related to just a single perspective—we know of the presence of air when it moves. But what other ways are there by which we can show that air is everywhere?

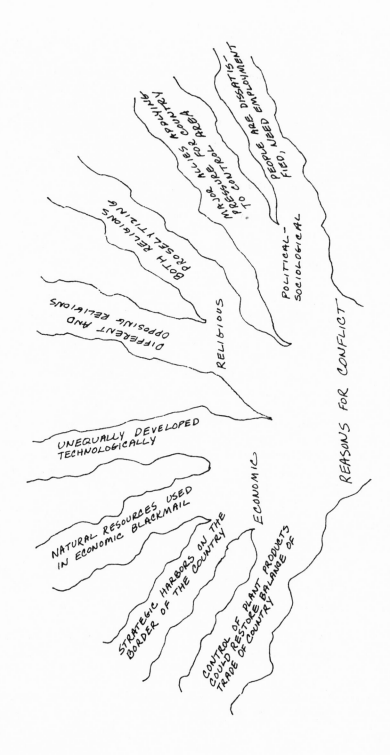

PEOPLE ARE DISSATIS-
FIED, NEED EMPLOYMENT

MAJOR ALLIES APPLYING
PRESSURE FOR COUNTRY
TO CONTROL AREA

POLITICAL-
SOCIOLOGICAL

BOTH RELIGIONS
PROSELYTIZING

DIFFERENT AND
OPPOSING RELIGIONS

RELIGIOUS

UNEQUALLY DEVELOPED
TECHNOLOGICALLY

NATURAL RESOURCES USED
IN ECONOMIC BLACKMAIL

STRATEGIC HARBORS ON THE
BORDER OF THE COUNTRY

CONTROL OF PLANT PRODUCTS
COULD RESTORE BALANCE OF
TRADE OF COUNTRY

ECONOMIC

REASONS FOR CONFLICT

Idea Tree

For example, what about air in closed places? Some of the ideas offered in answer to this question are:

- A blown-up balloon, when popped, expels air.
- If you place a bottle in water in such a way as to keep the water out, when you tip the bottle the air will come out of it in bubbles.
- If you suck in, you can fill your lungs with air; when you blow out, you know that there is air still inside you.

Still other questions that might be asked to change a group's perspective on air are:

- What about chemical reactions with air in controlling fires?
- What about the need for air to support life?

Here is another example of the application of this technique:
You ask your class to design an unusual package for cookies. These are a few of the ideas that are suggested:

- a rolling pin filled with cookies
- a package with a picture of a mother to suggest home-baked cookies
- a package with a cover on which there is a child's smiling face
- a package shaped like a cookie jar.

Though you naturally welcome these ideas, the problem is they all come from the same set—cookies as food. You redirect the thinking of the class—what about cookies as something else? A number of the suggestions you get in answer to this question include:

- cookies as airplane cargo
- a cookie necklace
- a book package in which the cookies are integrated into the pictures
- a circus wagon filled with animal cookies
- cookies as the wheels of an automobile.

5. Look for puzzling facts or events.[16]

Puzzles, discrepancies, or ambiguous situations frequently confuse us, conflict with what we think will happen, or don't seem to fit into normal patterns. Yet learning to make puzzles and discrepancies work for us can be one of the most challenging problems in the development of creative thinking.

People can have a difficult time even recognizing that a discrepancy exists, since they tend to take many things for granted and often accept puzzling occurrences as a matter of course. Often, too, they don't take the time to observe things carefully enough or to "tease out" the discrepancies. One famous person who knew the importance of being sensitive to puzzling or unexplained phenomena which others took for granted was Albert Einstein. When asked how he arrived at his ideas, he replied that they resulted from his "inability to understand the obvious."

Still another reason why puzzles and discrepancies often go unrecognized is that they may be the result of a mistake which someone wants to hide or forget. But mistakes can also be used to advantage. One example of this is Sir Alexander Fleming's experience with a "green mold" (later called penicillin) that "mistakenly" got into his bacteria cultures. Two other scientists had also observed the green mold in similar "accidents," but neither had paid close enough attention to the "accident" and so never discovered its importance.

Making productive use of puzzles and discrepancies requires that you actively look for them, that you try to make sense out of them, and that you eventually formulate an explanation or theory which will reasonably account for their existence. Although this last step is the ultimate one in the creative process, in the case of young children you will probably find it more productive to devote most of your attention to the first two steps.

Present your pupils with puzzling situations and sensitize them to view such situations as potential sources of interesting questions and creative solutions. Stimulate their curiosity in a wide variety of subjects. Help them to explain the "mysteries" they may encounter by introducing them to many of the techniques presented in this model. And, finally, encourage them to consider many different solutions to a problem before they arrive at the "correct" solution.

Examples of puzzling phenomena can be frequently be found in the newspapers, sometimes in the form of headlines: "Jupiter Riddle—Planet's magnetic field shows unexpected shift"; "Unexpected 60-foot hole found in homeowner's backyard." Or they may appear in reports such as the following one: "There have been recent disputes as to whether low-cholesterol diets prevent heart diseases. A statistician, comparing groups who followed strict health regimens with those who didn't, claimed that he found no statistically significant difference between groups."

6. Explore your thinking through subtraction and reversal.[17]

There are several ways of getting your students to change their thinking so that their ideas become more productive or creative. Subtraction is one method. Taking away one aspect of a product has often resulted in the creation of a new product. For example:

- telegraph—wire = wireless telegraph
- horse-drawn carriage—horse = horseless carriage
- picture taking—lengthy development process = Polaroid
- lamp—switch = touch lamp
- socks—heel = tube socks

"Taking away" the need for a solution can also often solve a problem. Here is an example. The way this problem was originally posed was as follows: "How can an eraser be made to last the life of a pencil?" So-called normal solutions might seem to lie in the direction of developing a more durable or larger eraser. However, "taking away" the need for erasers by asking oneself the question, "Must one have an eraser to erase?" might lead one to wonder whether pencil marks could be made to disappear if they were rubbed a certain way or exposed to certain kinds of light. It is even possible that people's attitudes could be changed to the point where they would be prepared to accept the visibility of mistakes.

"Reversal" is another method for changing people's thinking. An interesting reversal technique is illustrated by Aesop's fable about the crow and the pitcher of water. The thirsty crow wishes to get a drink of water from a pitcher but the water level is so low he cannot reach it. Instead of trying to get his beak far enough down to reach the water (an impossibility in any case), the clever crow considers whether there is a way he can bring the water level up. He successfully solves the problem by dropping stones in the pitcher until the water level is high enough for him to satisfy his thirst.

Reversal techniques often call for changing the direction of relationships. In some relationships, one thing acts upon or affects another thing in a particular way. Thus the teacher teaches the students; fishermen catch fish; rain affects plant growth. What would happen, though, if school were set up so that pupils taught teachers? How would the idea of fish catching fisherman affect the question of fishing equipment? (How, for example, was such a reversal of relationships used by Hemingway in his *Old Man and the Sea*?) Could a device be created whose effect would be that plant growth could influence the amount of rainfall? By using some imagination, you can no doubt come up with similar examples of your own.

7. Put yourself in another person's shoes.[18]

Not only does this technique help one to understand the actions and feelings of other people, but it can also be useful in the designing of machines, equipment, and facilities. Role playing is one of the more useful methods for learning "to feel what it's like to be someone else." Here are some examples of possible role-playing activities:

- Design clothes for a person who lives alone and is confined to a wheelchair.
- Help Jim, who got lost in the woods at night while on a backpacking trip.
- Role-play the following scene: Two soldiers—one from the North who has lost a brother in the Civil War, the other from the South whose home and city have been burned down—meet in a western town where they have both gone to start a new life.

8. Work backwards (Just suppose).[19]

The well-known puzzle of the three fishermen whose lines got tangled is commonly used to illustrate the wisdom of working backwards. A fish is discovered attached to one of the three lines. The problem is to figure out which fisherman caught the fish. The solution can be found more easily if the problem solver starts with the fish instead of the fishermen.

Mathematicians have often made important discoveries by arriving at insightful solutions to problems, and then working backwards to trace the logical steps that led to the solutions. Similarly, debaters often begin by taking a position and then looking for arguments to support that position.

When employing a "just suppose" approach, one starts with a far-fetched idea and, by "supposing," works backwards in the hope of making that speculation a real possibility. Trying to make "imagined impossibilities" work has resulted on numerous occasions in highly original and effective ideas and products. And, even if the idea turns out to be really impossible, it can often lead to other "impossible" ideas that turn out to be useful.

Many inventions exist today because someone "supposed" something and then persisted until he or she made that idea work. Computers, tape recorders, the optacon—all were considered "impossible" at the time they were conceived. In the literary field, too, we marvel at the prophetic accuracy of the "just suppose" novels of someone like Jules Verne.

Here are a number of examples of possible activities that will help your students to "work backwards":

- Ask your pupils to solve a mystery by "supposing the impossible." You can start, for example, by citing a real or imagined account of a robbery. The children will have fun "just supposing" that the missing loot is hidden in an impossible place—and then, by working backwards, making up stories about how it might have gotten there.
- Make a list of some "impossible" but potentially useful ideas. Have the class "just suppose" that people could live underwater, that blind people could see without using their eyes, that people could learn while

sleeping, etc. Then have them do some research to see if any progress has actually been made in turning these "impossible" ideas into reality.

• Have the class think of some "impossible" machine (e.g., a machine to harness the energy of ocean currents, a machine enabling deaf mutes to hear and speak). Then let them try to design it. Or ask students to suppose the words "a," "the," and "an" did not exist, and then write a paragraph without using any of these words.

9. Make predictions and consider consequences (Guess what's going to happen).[20]

Some unusual ideas and images can also occur when, instead of working backwards, one "leaps forward" so to speak by making predictions and then considering the consequences. You can stimulate this kind of thinking in your students by using either hypothetical or real situations. For example:

- What will happen if the growth in population, consumption, and pollution continues at its present rate?
- What would have to be created or changed if people were to dance on their hands rather than their feet?
- How would life be different if there were no more trees? No more automobiles? No more machines?
- What would happen if robots did all the work for people?
- What might happen if we discover a way to support life on the moon? On Mars?
- What would happen if the Mississippi River were suddenly stopped at its source?

10. Use analogies to make the strange familiar.
11. Use analogies to make the familiar strange.[21]

Analogies are excellent tools for stimulating creativity in a classroom. With this in mind, W. J. J. Gordon developed an analogy system for creative learning which he calls the synectics system. By using this system, children can explore and discover new relationships between objects, events, concepts, or even feelings.

In synectics, one uses analogies to "make the familiar strange" by discovering a new context within which one can view familiar phenomena. On the other hand, one "makes the strange familiar" by relating one's current knowledge to unfamiliar phenomena. In short, analogy-making can be thought of as a wordplay technique, in which words (and the ideas behind the words) are manipulated.

The synectics system devised by Gordon uses three types of analogies:

1. *Direct analogy.* This type of analogy involves a simple comparison of two objects (A giraffe is like jello because . . .). The relationship between the two objects can be close (obvious) or it can be distant (strained). The usefulness of the analogy is generally dependent upon the amount of distance or strain that exists within the comparison. For example, either a school or a coral reef could be made analogous to a family. However, since the school provides a more obvious analogy, according to Gordon the analogy of the coral reef is likely to be a more productive direction to take.

2. *Personal analogy.* This type of analogy involves a description of the feelings that result from one's efforts to identify with another person, a concept, a plant, an animal, or an object (Be the thing! Be a pen!). The identification that occurs when techniques like role playing are used tends to involve the whole entity (event, person, idea, etc.); in personal analogy, however, the identification often occurs *not* with the whole, but only with a part. Thus, instead of identifying with the man (the whole) who has a cold, one might identify either with the cold virus in his nose or with the nose itself (a part). It can also be productive at times to have the class identify with inorganic objects. For example, ask students to try to think like an electron, like the desert sand in a wind storm, etc.

3. *Compressed conflict.* This analogy system calls for the use of seemingly incompatible word pairs, i.e., an impenetrable sieve, a happy defeat, etc. Compressed conflict requires one to compose a poetic, two-word summary of a phenomenon or situation. A compressed conflict phrase is developed by using either personal or direct analogy to find those characteristics of an object which appear to be incompatible and in logical conflict.

According to W. J. J. Gordon, compressed conflict is often a means for expressing intuitive feelings that may have promising experimental possibilities. As an example of this phenomenon, he cites Louis Pasteur's talk of "safe attack" that preceded his experiments with antitoxins.[22]

Of the three types of analogies, compressed conflict tends to provide the broadest insight into a subject. Since it demands a strong grasp of the logical relationships between words, it is probably better to employ it with older pupils who are experienced with analogy techniques.

The following are some examples of analogies that can be used as tools when exploring a variety of subject areas:

- Are there any analogies to the batik technique in which wax is painted on cloth? What are they? (Examples: suntan lotion, waterproofing.)
- What kind of associations do certain sounds bring to your mind?
- Explore "being" a certain sound or combination of sounds. How will your body move?
- How is war like a cup of tea? Making friends like a truck?

6
The Experiential Learning Model

This model[1] can provide children with classroom opportunities to learn and develop logical thinking skills. It is based on the assumption that children learn best when they are offered experiences that are appropriate to their particular level of development as well as materials that will pique their curiosity and require of them some physical manipulation.

Introduction

PART 1   Classroom Examples

PART 2   Procedures for Using the Experiential Learning Model in the Classroom

PART 3   Settings Needed When Using the Experiential Learning Model

PART 4   Anticipated Student Outcomes of Using the Experiential Learning Model

PART 5   Checklists for Evaluating a Program Based on the Experiential Learning Model

PART 6   References and Resources

Appendix

Introduction

The experiential learning model is based in large part on the cognitive development theories of the late Swiss psychologist Jean Piaget. In terms of this model, children's interactions with their environment are viewed as the primary method by which they discover knowledge and develop thinking skills. The teacher's job is to provide them with experiences appropriate to their particular stage of development and to help them learn how to interpret or generalize from these experiences.

What is intelligence? How does it develop? What assists or retards its development? In attempting to answer such questions, Piaget evolved a theory of human development that has influenced the field of education.

According to Piaget, intelligence is a complex system of mental operations for processing and organizing the "messages" which a person constantly receives from his or her environment. This system, he says, develops in four stages:

1. the sensorimotor stage   0–2 years
2. the preoperational stage   2–7 years
3. the concrete operational stage   7–11 years
4. the formal operational stage   11 years to adulthood

Every child passes through these stages in the same order, although at different rates of speed. The stages are hierarchical; that is, one cannot arrive at a more advanced stage until one has completed all the earlier stages.

A child's movement from stage to stage is dependent upon *maturation* (which determines the range of possibilities within each stage), upon *interaction with the social and physical environment* (which accounts for a realization of these possibilities), and upon a mechanism which Piaget calls *equilibration* (which can roughly be defined as an individual's need to maintain a state of equilibrium as he or she interacts with the environment).

As the child proceeds through each stage, he or she develops three classes of knowledge:

1. logical-mathematical knowledge
2. social knowledge
3. physical knowledge.

(A more detailed explanation of the stages and other components of Piaget's theory can be found in the Appendix of this model, pp. 158–164.)

As in the case of all influential theorists, Piaget's ideas have generated controversy within the fields of education and psychology. Because his ideas are complex, and because he himself did not indicate exactly how they ought to be translated into educational practice, various interpretations exist of how his theory can most effectively be applied to the classroom situation.

The experiential learning model described in the pages that follow is constructed from those components of developmental theory which have been tested in the classroom and are now part of the educational literature. Though the influence of Piaget on this model is undoubtedly great, acknowledgment must also be made here to many others who have developed systematic procedures based upon careful study and interpretation of the nature of child development. In Part 6: References and Resources (pp. 157–158) we have indicated the many sources from which this model has been drawn.

Assumptions of the experiential learning model

1. *Instruction should encourage the development of each child's thinking processes in logical-mathematical, social, and physical areas rather than the mere acquisition of information.* The elementary school years are critical in the development of a person's thinking ability. During these formative years individuals mature to the point where those operations which characterize general intelligence become readily available to them. During these years children learn "how to learn." To help them strengthen their intellectual ability to interact productively with their environment, a teacher must be able to distinguish between those experiences that will help them to develop their overall intelligence and those that will merely result in the acquisition of information.

Since, as Piaget has indicated, intelligence at any stage is a complex system of mental operations for processing and organizing incoming data, his three-part classification of knowledge—logical-mathematical, social, and physical—provides the teacher with useful insights into the development of these operations among children of elementary school age. It also suggests directions that curriculum development can take. In the area of logical-mathematical knowledge, for example, a curriculum should be devised that provides adequate practice in such operations as classification, seriation, numerical and spatial concepts, and temporal relationships. In the area of social knowledge, the curriculum should help the child to move from egocentric to sociocentric thought, while in the area of physical knowledge, he or she should be assisted in developing a clear understanding of the predictability of the physical world.

2. *Since learning is most effective when children are interacting with the environment, the learning activities a teacher schedules should grow out of their individual interests and experiences.* Activities of this kind should pique children's curiosity and actively involve them. It matters little whether these activities are called work or play. The distinction between work and play is in any case an artificial one, since a child at play is a child working at learning.

Activities that help children develop their general intelligence have two characteristics: They call for the children's *active* involvement rather than their passive acceptance, and they lead children to question their existing views.

In this connection, it is worth pointing out that the drill or paper-and-pencil activities that are so often the "work" of many classrooms achieve neither of these goals, while many activities that are normally thought of as "play" achieve both. In planning their learning activities, then, teachers should eliminate the work-play distinction from their thinking together with the assumption that the former leads to learning whereas the latter does not.[2]

Teachers should likewise recognize that activities should grow out of a child's interests and experiences. If, for example, the purpose of an activity is to give a child practice in classification, it doesn't matter what objects he or she classifies—rocks, dinosaurs, foods, cards, types of stories, or fictional characters. Similarly, a child can practice computational skills in a variety of ways—by playing monopoly, by computing the cost of constructing a soap box derby entry, by taking charge of the class's field trip finances, etc. In fact, a child can develop concepts of measurement in a sandbox better than out of a workbook. And it is all to the better if he or she learns to read while seeking information or entertainment rather than by being put to work on a set of programmed readers.

3. *The role of the teacher should not merely be to transmit information but rather to provide a variety of concrete materials for the children to manipulate, to allow and encourage them to work with and learn from one another, and to assist them in their efforts to assimilate information from their environment by asking them questions which will help them to think about and interpret their experiences.* Children process (mentally act upon) the information they receive from the environment and make it their own. In this way, they develop the intellectual structures that allow them to interact with their environment in an even more efficient manner. This being the case, the teacher must pay special attention both to what constitutes the children's environment and to what they do with it.

The classroom environment should be carefully structured and be filled with interesting and challenging materials for the students. Since most elementary school children are either in the preoperational or concrete operational stage of development, the more concrete the materials, the more likely it is that they will learn from them. For example, if children are to learn about volume, they should be allowed to play with liquids. If they are to understand how a flower grows, they should plant the seed, care for it, and then watch it grow. If they are to learn about "community helpers," the teacher must extend the school environment *beyond* the classroom walls. Children should be taken to the city dump or fire station where they can actively explore the garbage or fire truck, where they can ask the questions to which they want answers. Then, and only then should they attempt to build models, draw pictures, or in some other way reproduce and record those things about the experience which they took away with them.

Peers are a vital part of a child's learning environment, in terms of both cognitive and social learning. According to Piaget, children begin to question their own views when they seem different from the views of others. Of course, if the differences are too great, children may simply dismiss these differences and hold instead to their original conceptions. That is why a younger child can sometimes learn a concept more easily from an older child than from an adult. (It should be obvious in this connection that while a five-year-old should not be sent to play baseball with a group of nine- and ten-year-olds, there are very good reasons for asking a seven-year-old to work, for example, on a science project with an eight- or nine-year-old.)

Teachers, it is worth noting, are not simply providers of materials for the children; far more, they are a crucial part of the children's environment. Therefore, teachers should be constantly interacting with their students. They should not only help them find activities and peer-group arrangements which actively involve them, but encourage them to observe the effects of their actions on others. Furthermore, if this model is to be used successfully, teachers must be able to ask children the right questions, to observe their actions, and to listen attentively to their answers. Finally, they must develop a willingness to let the children experience their environment in their own way so that they can truly profit from their actions and experiences.

According to Piaget, the thinking of children differs significantly from the thinking of adults. So when asking a child a question, teachers should not be listening for the "right" or "wrong" answer. Instead, they should be listening for clues that can tell them, for example, which operations of the children are inadequate and therefore limit their grasp of an idea or concept. A child can hardly be expected to handle addition problems without first mastering certain seriation and classification operations. Similarly, for children to know that $1 + 2 = 3$, they must also know the order of 1, 2, 3 (that 2 is more than 1 and, at the same time, less than 3), and that $2 = 1 + 1$ and $3 = 1 + 1 + 1$. One cannot assume that children are able to perform these operations merely because they can count.

How can teachers find out the way a child thinks? Well, they can ask the child to work with some materials and then to explain or describe what occurred. "Show me" must be as important a part of the classroom vocabulary as "Tell me." And asking children such questions as "What is happening?" and "Why don't you tell me about it?" helps them to describe the world as it appears to them.

Teachers should also be aware of the difficulty children may have in trying to answer questions that may arise while they are in the process of learning concrete operations. The answers to these questions often have to do with forces of nature, physical laws, and scientific theories which children do not yet understand.[3] Although they can be taught to memorize appropriate answers, all they learn is how to memorize—little more. A child who has just conducted an experiment in which he dissolves salt in water cannot answer the question "Why does the salt dissolve?" However, he can answer questions that grow out of his perceptual orientation and build upon it: "Where did the salt go? Where is it now? How can you tell? How do we get the salt back? What other things look and feel like salt? What would happen if you did the same thing to sugar?" etc.

Nothing is more crucial than for teachers to *listen* to children. The questions children ask as well as the answers they give often reveal if and when they are trying to assimilate new information and to accommodate their thinking to it. It is most important, therefore, that teachers encourage such student questioning. To ensure that it occurs, they should provide a stimulating atmosphere and take care to see that a child's questions are not belittled. They can also point out relationships between what the child already knows and what he is learning; they can help the child acquire appropriate language so he or she can express ideas clearly; and, through appropriate questioning strategies, they can lead the child to organize and clarify his or her thought processes.

Part 1: Classroom Examples

"For Piaget, good schooling involves presenting the child with situations in which he himself experiments; that is, manipulates things, manipulates symbols, poses questions, and seeks his own answers, reconciling what he finds at one time with what he finds at another, and comparing his findings with those of other children."[4]

An extended description of a class taught by Ms. Adams and a shorter description of Ms. Webb's class appear below.

Example 1

Ms. Adams' class. At an elementary school in Los Angeles, Ms. Adams teaches a combined second- and third-grade class. Some of her activities and materials are planned in concert with Ms. Smith, the teacher in the next classroom who has a combined K-1 class. The door between the two rooms is always kept open and the children are allowed to go back and forth for various activities. Since Ms. Smith has expertise in the piano, most of the musical games and activities take place in her room.

There are two other doors in Ms. Adams' classroom. One opens onto a play yard; the other onto the hallway. Both doors are generally kept open. In addition to outdoor play equipment, the play yard has easels, paints, and clay materials for the use of both classes. As for the hallway, it contains various displays of the children's work.

Originally the hallway was the site of a "grocery store" constructed by Ms. Adams' class which had shelves made of cardboard boxes and which was stocked with empty packages brought from home. Having the children arrange the shelves whenever a "new shipment" arrived (i.e., when there were sufficient donations from home to restock the shelves) provided good classification and seriation activities.

The construction of the store grew out of a class visit to a neighborhood grocery store on the day of its weekly delivery. In addition to questioning the grocer and watching him at work, the children were allowed to help by pricing and then shelving some of the goods. As "payment," they were given several empty cardboard boxes (which they subsequently used to build their own store), an old order book containing a comprehensive list of merchandise complete with purchase prices, and a large bag of assorted fruit which Ms. Adams dispensed at lunchtime over the next few days.

The visit to the grocery store also served as a springboard for several weeks of activities in math (food prices, family budgets, unit pricing, etc.), science (food families and nutrition), social studies (money as a unit of exchange, the provision of food in a society), ethical development (discussion of stealing and its consequences—an outgrowth of the grocer's answers to questions put to him by the children), language arts (letters of thanks to the grocer and stories about the visit), reading (stories about food and related subjects), and art (drawings and painting of the visit, as well as designs and labels for new products).

Actually, Ms. Adams had not planned to teach a grocery unit this particular semester. The idea arose during the first few weeks while the children were getting acquainted with one another, and after it was discovered that the little grocery store (within walking distance of the school) was owned by the parents of one of the children.

If one were to observe Ms. Adams' classroom, one would note that the children are seated according to no special arrangement. Instead, the room is organized by area, and the children move from one area to another, working at different tasks—either individually or in small groups. It is not uncommon, either, to see some children serving as tutors to others. As a result, the classroom is hardly a quiet one.

In one area are weighing, measuring, and counting implements, as well as a wide variety of materials—buttons, beads, water, etc.—for the children to measure, count, and weigh. There are also number lines of various kinds, Cuisenaire rods, and a big box of geometric blocks.

In the library area are comfortable chairs and many books on many subjects. There are also various sets of readers, but there is no one set for the entire class.

Next to the library area there is a writing table with paper and pencils, letter and number models, and boxes of illustrated word groups. One box contains animal names, sounds, and homes; another contains color, size, and shape words; a third contains simple action words. Some children who have volunteered are busy assembling additional boxes—one on dinosaurs and one on rockets, for example. All around the classroom are signs which clearly indicate areas and activities, while on the bulletin board there are sign-up sheets and assignment sheets.

In a cupboard that stands open along the wall there is a variety of arts and crafts materials—construction paper, colored pencils, crayons, bits of fabric, yarn, large darning needles, paste, etc. In still another part of the room are live goldfish, mice, and hamsters. The children are responsible for the care and upkeep of these animals.

There is a special "game" corner where the children can play chess, checkers, Monopoly, or a variety of teacher-made games involving matching words to pictures, as well as seriation, classification, and logical thinking tasks. Some of the games require adult supervision; some can be played alone; others require two or more players.

There is one table filled with collections of shells, leaves, nuts, etc. There are name tags, too, which enable the children to match items as well as short sentence descriptions of each item in the collection. The children will add other collectibles to this table as the semester progresses. On a second table there is a sign that reads "To Share with the Class." An assortment of items can be found here on any given day.

Miscellaneous items scattered about the room include: an old standard typewriter; a large box of old clothes for playacting; an assortment of hammers, saws, nails; remnants of wood; and a full-length mirror (for body movement activities and for the development of certain math and geometric concepts).

Against the far wall is a set of shelves—one for each child. Here the children keep their work and their accounts of what they have done. For example, the children each have an individual "word" book in which they record the new words they have learned to write and read. Similarly, after completing an activity, they each record their experiences on a set of summary cards. These cards are then placed in their own shoebox file on one of the shelves.

Though many of the classroom materials were assembled before the semester began, the children and parent volunteers are constantly replenishing supplies. Most of the materials were not purchased; they were donated, borrowed, made, or assembled by the teacher, the children, or the parents.

Parents are very important to the functioning of Ms. Adams' classroom. Since the children are working at a variety of tasks, additional adult assistance is useful—to help a child with an activity; to organize, repair, or replenish materials; to answer questions; to "play a game" with a child. Furthermore, children at these ages are still very much home-oriented, and they take great pleasure in having a parent come to school as a teacher aide or participant in their activities. And, of course, parental assistance gives Ms. Adams more time to attend to her own crucial tasks.

The class has spent the first few weeks of the semester getting acquainted—with each other, with Ms. Adams, with the classroom, and with the materials. Ms. Adams constantly encourages the children to talk about themselves, their families, their likes and dislikes. She takes an active part in these activities, telling the class about herself and her own preferences. At the same time, she introduces the children to the various areas in the room and explains the procedures for working with particular materials.

It does not take long for a routine to become established: A child comes into the room in the morning, checks to see if his or her name is on one of the "Responsibilities" lists (feeding the animals, for example), attends to that responsibility, and then proceeds to an activity of his or her own choosing. Most of the morning will be spent on individual and small group activities.

Throughout the day Ms. Adams works with the children on language development. She has a list of certain syntactical structures that aid logical thinking.[5] From this list she selects one daily and incorporates it into her own speech pattern while attempting to elicit the appropriate structure from the children as they go about their activities. This modeling and eliciting process is conducted in a natural, conversational manner. Ms. Adams also helps the children to incorporate the appropriate vocabulary into their explanations of what they are doing and observing as they work with the materials. (See Figure 21, Ms. Adams' Basic Vocabulary List.)

As the children work, Ms. Adams circulates among them, helping some of them to select activities or groups to work with, helping others to find answers to questions as they work with the materials, and conducting informal evaluations.

To demonstrate their comprehension of a concept, Ms. Adams has them manipulate the appropriate materials and then explain or describe

Figure 21. Ms. Adams' Basic Vocabulary List[6]

Words to Master				
first	tall	part	set	in front of
second	taller	whole	group	in back of
third	tallest		collection	next to
fourth		less	number	by
fifth	high	least		on top of
	low		next	beneath
small		same	last	below
smaller	narrow	different		above
smallest	wide		shape	close
	fat	as many as	size	up against
big	skinny	more than	length	opposite
bigger		less than	width	across from
biggest	some	just enough		the other side
	most		circle	the same side
long	all	put with	square	
longer	more	put together	rectangle	
longest	many	take away	triangle	before
	few	take apart		after
short			left	
shorter			right	
shortest				

NOTE: Ms. Adams feels that mastery of the words on this list is an essential prerequisite to many of the logical-mathematical activities.

what they have done. She knows that a child's ability to use certain words does not necessarily mean that he or she understands the underlying concepts. For this reason she keeps an informal diary to assist her in recalling significant incidents concerning the children. She also has a standard form that she fills out weekly to diagnose each child's needs and to evaluate the learning process. The information on the weekly forms, together with the children's work and the records they themselves keep become subjects of discussion at parent conferences. The children receive no grades. (The standard form is shown in Figure 22.[7])

It is worth noting that although Ms. Adams completes a form containing several categories for each child each week, she doesn't feel it is necessary for a child to engage in learning activities in each category each

---

Figure 22. Standard Form for Weekly Activities

Child's name _____   Week of _____

 I. Logical-mathematical knowledge

   A. Classification

   B. Seriation

   C. Number-Space

 II. Physical knowledge

 III. Social knowledge and personal development

   A. Communication skills

   B. Peer relations

   C. Sense of mastery

   D. Responsibility

---

week. Instead, a child may spend the better part of a week on one project, to the virtual exclusion of all else. Ms. Adams does feel, however, that a balance in the child's activities over a given semester is desirable, and she will therefore direct children to specific areas as she comes to know them and determines their needs.

Shortly before the morning break, Ms. Adams will call the children together as a group and conduct class business. Again after lunch, the class will come together for group activities—singing, discussions, play acting for problem solving, sharing things, story telling, group games, outdoor activities, etc.

As the children work together, problems, of course, arise from time to time. These problems become the subjects for group discussions and play-acting activities. But because the children are very often working on tasks of their own choosing, the disciplinary problems that result from resistance to an assigned task are kept to a minimum.

Example 2

Ms. Webb's class.[8] At the Lady Margaret Junior School outside of London, a class of nine- and ten-year-olds (of average intelligence), undertook the building of a duck pond. The catalyst for this project was the arrival of some ducklings among the school's livestock supply and the absence of any water place for them. Neither the teacher nor the children had ever done anything like this before.

In the exploratory phase of this project the children consulted their parents for information and brought books to class (including a catalogue from a gardener's supply firm) to learn more about construction design, materials, drainage, and costs. Conflicting advice from the books made it necessary for them to work with averages and means in order to accurately compute quantities and costs.

The next step—selection of the exact location—required a visit to the duck pond site with a surveyor's plan of the school in hand. At this point the children were divided into three working groups. Each group was given the task of measuring the yard and its contents in order to make scale plans—one for the class, one for the headmaster, and one for the rest of the school. (The measurements were eventually compared and were found to be very close to one another.)

This three-group arrangement was generally maintained throughout the project, although the compositions of the groups did vary as the work progressed—particularly since the first group to go to the yard on a given day consisted of the first ten children whose work on the pond was up to date.

As the project moved ahead, the children were introduced to concepts having to do with drainage, with the properties of water, cement, and brick, as well as with perimeter, area, angles, and measurement. Weather conditions and their effects on the work posed problems that had to be dealt with. Rules determining the requirements for working on the pond were evolved and adhered to. And an appreciation for the complexity of such a project was also developed. In the words of one of the children, "I learnt that it wasn't as easy as it looked."

The children kept a record of the project in the form of two books—one for their daily use in the class, and one to be used as the official record of the project. These books consisted of a written account of each step in the project, scaled-down versions of the plans, and other appropriate diagrams. The covers of the two books were chosen on the basis of a class competition to select the best design.

According to Ms. Webb, the learning resulting from the project was extensive. It included the following:

- increased understanding of math and science vocabulary
- growth in the ability to use measurement and construction tools
- increased ability to apply basic math and science concepts in practical situations
- production of artistic interpretations (in pictures and written form)
- development of interest in ducks and in the history of building
- increased feelings of confidence and self-reliance in the class as a whole
- improved interpersonal relationships within the class.

And, of course, the school now has a duck pond.

Part 2: Procedures for Using the Experiential Learning Model in the Classroom

In order to facilitate the use of the experiential learning model, here are some common questions you are likely to ask. These are followed by detailed answers and suggestions.

Getting started

1. *How well do I have to know the characteristics of each stage of a child's development in order to use this model successfully?* The more you know about how children's intellectual development occurs, and what your children

can and cannot do, the better you will be able to work with them. As an experienced classroom teacher, you undoubtedly have discovered for yourself many of the principles that will be briefly described here. You know, for example, that children love to touch and feel, to poke and press, and in general to handle things. What you may not have known is that this behavior is their primary mode of learning until approximately the age of eleven. (You can find further information on the intellectual characteristics of preoperational and concrete operational children in the annotated references.)

2. *Relying so much upon the children's own choice of activities and materials may represent quite a departure from my former teaching style. How can I make the change comfortably?* You needn't change everything you do all at once. Begin slowly by selecting one subject for which there are already published guidelines or curricula.[9] Or begin by organizing your room into areas where children can go to work on freely chosen special projects, either individually or in small groups, during a special time of the day.

Planning a curriculum

1. *Can I use this model with a traditional curriculum that is organized by subject?* Yes, you can. You will find, however, that frequently you will turn to math and science activities for the development of logical thinking skills. You will also find that a single activity may result in growth in several areas (Interesting projects cause children to seek out further information and foster their desire to communicate artistically and verbally. Recall in this connection Ms. Webb's description of the learning that resulted from building the duck pond.)

2. *Is there a Piagetian curriculum?* Though Piaget himself did not devise a curriculum, various educators have tried to organize curricula based on his learning theory, especially in the subject areas of math and science. In fact, much of Ms. Adams' curriculum could be described as "Piagetian." (For other examples of Piagetian goals, see Part 4, Anticipated Student Outcomes of Using the Experiential Learning Model.)

3. *What about reading?* In American elementary schools, reading scores are often looked upon as the primary measure of a child's accomplishment. Yet few people would say that the major goal of our schools is to get the child to make a high score on reading tests. Rather, reading should be regarded as a necessary and marvelously satisfying tool that every child should acquire at some point in his or her elementary school experience. Reading, defined this way, depends upon the totality of the child's social, physical, and logical-mathematical knowledge. A

curriculum that helps a child develop his or her intellectual processes will at the same time create the desire to read.

4.. *This model seems to be heavily cognitive or intellectual in its emphasis. Can it also contribute to the affective portion of a curriculum?* When using the model, you will attempt to provide a classroom environment in which

- the child's interests are respected and deemed valuable
- the child is encouraged to ask questions and to feel that no question is foolish or stupid
- the child is encouraged to feel that he or she has the ability to learn the answers to questions
- the child is listened to by teachers and peers
- the child participates with others in activities that are both interesting and challenging.

Unless the child's personal problems fall outside the normal range, a classroom environment such as this will lead to his or her personal and intellectual growth. In addition, by creating a classroom environment in which the child is encouraged and taught how to work with others, social learning is certain to flourish.

Evaluation

1. *What about report cards?* When using this model, you will find that traditional report cards seem to be an unsuitable tool for presenting information on pupil progress. Parents will be better informed about their child's progress if you confer with them directly, using anecdotal records and the child's own work as the basis for this discussion.

2. *How do I explain to parents that their child is not doing the same things that they did when they were in school?* It may be that this model is a new one in your school. Until recently, class texts and workbooks were the prime means of instruction, and standardized tests were the important measure of a school's accomplishments. However, even without such a rigid structure in your school, you still may have parents who want to know why their child is not bringing home a workbook every day, or why class time was used for making cookies, for example. In responding to questions of this kind, try to

- discuss with the parents the goals you have in mind for their child. Explain, if necessary, the theory of child development which underlies these goals and the activities provided. Parents will be more likely to accept the baking of cookies as an educational activity if they understand that the child is in reality learning about fractions and proportions while he or she is figuring out the ingredients necessary to provide everyone in class with an appropriate number of cookies.

• involve the parents. Ask them to help prepare materials, to come to class and work with the children, to organize and help with field trips, etc.

• get parents to observe their children at home and to talk with them about school activities. The child who enjoys school and is interested in learning is walking testimony that an experiential classroom "works."

3. *Is there any standardized test I can use that addresses itself to Piagetian objectives?* Goldschmid and Bentler have developed such a test called the *Concept Assessment Kit—Conservation.* It is an individual test which seeks to determine if a child can recognize that "certain properties, such as substance, weight, volume, or numbers, remain unchanged in the face of certain transformations, such as changes in the object's form, shape, color, or position."[10]

Research is also under way on the development of a Piagetian Intelligence Test. For the most part, though, such a test will not really provide you with the kind of information you need. Therefore, you will probably have to develop your own diagnostic testing materials and procedures. Here are some suggestions for doing this:

• Begin with your objectives. State them in terms of pupil behavior, so that you know what to look for when you test.

• If possible, use materials in the test situation that are similar to those that you developed for teaching the concepts. If you have an abundance of materials, a child will certainly not have used them all.

• Develop standardized questioning techniques, so that a parent or classroom volunteer can help you work with each individual child. Asking a child to demonstrate proficiency with the materials and then to explain what he or she has done will tell you if the appropriate concepts have been understood.[11]

Part 3: Settings Needed When Using the Experiential Learning Model

Classroom organization

1. *To use this model successfully, should I have the help of other adults in the classroom?* Such help is useful, of course. But you can also use the model without it. Remember: Among your best resources are the children themselves. Let them organize, arrange, and take care of classroom materials. Let them explain, demonstrate concepts, and work with one

another. In so doing, they are helping you as well as furthering their own learning. Use every opportunity to allow them to do things, even if in some instances you could do the tasks more quickly or efficiently yourself. (If you do decide to use other adults, give them a short introduction to what you are doing and why, so that they will know what to expect from your class.)

2. *Do I simply outfit the classroom with various interesting materials and activities and then set the children loose?* You can begin that way *if* you feel comfortable doing so. Some teachers, however, prefer more structure (Ms. Adams, for example). If you are such a person, the Nuffield math curriculum clearly spells out a procedure for introducing children to mathematics within the school environment. It suggests that the teacher begin by making children aware of the mathematical possibilities that lie in the most commonplace classroom objects, and then have them act on these possibilities by measuring the objects, arranging them, identifying them, etc. After that, the teacher can introduce new materials and even extend the environment to include the home and other areas of the school. When new materials are introduced in the classroom, children should be able to experiment freely with them and learn the appropriate vocabulary so that they can label them. The teacher can, at a later date, deal with any problems or confusions that may have arisen from the children's use of the materials.

Learning centers are one good way of organizing a classroom in which experiential learning principles are being employed, but they are not the only way. As a matter of fact, there is no one single correct way of organizing a classroom for the successful use of this model. What is essential, though, is that no matter how the classroom is arranged, the children engage in activities which involve their energies fully. Equally important is that these activities permit them to touch, manipulate, play with, and arrange a variety of concrete objects.

Selecting and developing materials and activities

1. *Are workbooks, programmed materials, and repetitive exercises a waste of time?* Some children enjoy and profit from the use of workbooks and similar materials. Many will seek out and learn from repetitive activities, while others will be bored by them. In any event, to use such activities and materials as the *primary* vehicle of instruction is to ignore two crucial tenets of this model: 1) if the child is inattentive while engaging in an activity, he or she is *not* learning from it; 2) concepts taught through using a workbook can often be better demonstrated by the use of concrete, manipulable materials.

2. *Does "active" learning for the concrete operational child mean simply the manipulation of concrete objects?* Active learning calls for both physical and mental activity. Whenever possible, therefore, children should be involved physically by feeling, touching, smelling, seeing. But, since the children are also manipulating words, ideas, and relationships, ask them to reflect on and describe in words their thinking process.

3. *Will I find that accumulating useful materials is costly?* Sets and kits of "Piagetian" materials are now being developed commercially. Since many of them are expensive, you need not buy them. You may wish however, to examine them, to "borrow" ideas, and even to purchase certain items or selected games that aren't too costly. Don't depend solely upon kits or commercial materials, however. Remember, the activities and materials you choose should relate directly to the particular interests of the children in your class. If a kit provides buttons to be used in classification activities, there will undoubtedly be a child who will discover other, more intriguing uses for those buttons. And even if this is not the case, that same child may love model cars and so be persuaded to classify them instead of the buttons.

4. *Preparing materials and designing activities would appear to be time-consuming and complicated tasks. Are there any tips for making me more efficient?* The process of translating a curriculum into experiential learning activities and materials will stretch your own inventive capacities. But you will undoubtedly find that the more you do it, the easier and more fun it becomes. Besides there are ways of making it easier. Here are four examples:

• Do some research. Examine existing materials. Teacher resource centers and educational toy stores are good places in which to browse for new and interesting materials. "Borrow" the ideas of colleagues. You may find that those teachers who are the "favorites" of the children are the ones whose techniques provide children with opportunities to do and to experience. Finally, read and learn about successful projects or interesting classes.

• Begin with what you already have. Use your current workbooks and teacher manuals as starting points. Examine the suggested activities and materials, revising those which do not provide the correct answers to these questions: Will the activity pique the children's curiosity? Will it maintain their attention and interest? Can the demonstration or practice materials be made more concrete? (For example, if a unit in the math workbook is attempting to teach the identification and extension of number patterns, you might devise a game using objects—poker chips, perhaps—which will help a child to discover and visualize patterns.)

• Call upon the parents. Ask them for their ideas and suggestions, and have them help you create activities.

• Question your children. What are their favorite games? Their special interests? Do you have a group of boys who are particularly interested in baseball? If so, help them learn to compute batting averages after they have played a game. Teach them how to read the sports page. Let them compile lists of baseball vocabulary. Have them create a baseball Hall of Fame for the enjoyment of the other children. Teach them the basic geometry and physics involved in hitting a ball with a bat—angles, velocity, etc.

Part 4: Anticipated Student Outcomes of Using the Experiential Learning Model

When using this model, look for changes in two specific areas:

• *Children should develop a positive attitude toward school.* They should come to associate learning with activity, enjoyment, and stimulation, and to regard it as a social process in which their own views are questioned and tested against the views of others. They should see the school as a place where questions can be asked without fear of ridicule, where their interests and preferences are considered important, and where they can make choices of their own.

• *As a result of this program, the children should also develop processes of logical thinking.* They should develop observational skills and the ability to organize, classify, and see relationships in what they observe, so that they will have the necessary strategies for new learning.

In the following pages, you will find a set of objectives[12] that may well be of use to you as you plan your own program. Most of the objectives listed there are appropriate for the early elementary school years (K-3), when children are making the transition from preoperational to concrete operational thinking processes. Ms. Adams (the teacher presented earlier in the first classroom example) would be likely to use these as a basis for her instruction. The objectives we offer are intended as examples—representative, but not exhaustive of the possibilities available to you. We have written them at two levels of specificity: Program objectives in the left-hand column are general; the outcomes in the right-hand column spell out specifically related student behaviors.

Logical-mathematical operations

Program Objectives

Related Student Behaviors

The pupil will develop classification skills for organizing the environment and seeing relationships in it.

1. Identifies properties of objects (size, color, shape, etc.) and matches objects on the basis of more than one property
2. Selects from among objects one which will complete a set, keeping in mind two or more properties of the objects of the set
3. Combines objects to make up subclasses
4. Combines subclasses to make supraclasses
5. Recognizes the existence of complementary classes (the set that does *not* have the property of the specific class)
6. Changes from one criterion for grouping to another
7. Takes apart a whole class to find subclasses, and then makes comparisons of "all" and "some"
8. Discovers the intension and extension of a class (The intension of a class is the properties common to that class; the extension of a class is the inclusion of all objects or experiences possessing the common properties defined by its intension.)
9. Recognizes that an object has simultaneous membership in two classes
10. Puts together related elements from several groups
11. Makes all possible combinations of elements.

The pupil will develop problem-solving skills involving number, measurement, space, and seriation.

1. Uses his or her body to
   a. establish correspondence among parts of the body (equivalent sets, left-right symmetry)
   b. establish correspondence between the body and objects in the environment

Program Objectives

Related Student Behaviors

    c. compute
    d. organize space
    e. arrive at units of measurement
2. Matches numerical symbols with their names, and geometric shapes with their names
3. Duplicates and extends patterns made by objects arranged according to size, length, or geometric shape
4. Duplicates and extends sound patterns
5. Conserves discontinuous quantities[13] by
    a. establishing one-to-one correspondence
    b. recognizing sets with the same or different numerical properties
    c. manipulating numerical sets (either by joining two sets to create a new set or by separating and rejoining set members)
6. Separates into parts and recombines the parts of a geometric region
7. Conserves continuous quantities (water, sand, etc.)[14]
8. Visualizes how something will look when it is moved in space
9. Visualizes how something will look from another point of view
10. Orders objects or events according to one or two dimensions so that each object or event holds its place with respect to the preceding and following objects or events.

The pupil will develop an awareness of the regularities and predictability of the environment, living and nonliving.

1. Can use his or her body to observe and imitate sounds and movements of animals
2. Can recognize, identify, and describe the properties of animals, including:
    a. their physical features
    b. their habitats
    c. their methods of food procurement
    d. their social behavior

Program Objectives

Related Student Behaviors

3. Can group animals on the basis of the above categories (features, habitat, etc.)
4. Can identify similarities and differences between animals and humans on the basis of the above categories
5. Can classify objects by their properties (shape, color, texture, materials)
6. Can classify objects by the influence or effect they have on one another
7. Can classify objects by the patterns in which they can be arranged
8. Understands and correctly uses the words "object," "property," "material"
9. Describes accurately the properties of an object
10. Compares the properties of objects
11. Compares objects made of differing materials
12. Distinguishes between objects made of one material and objects made of several materials
13. Recognizes that an object's form or appearance can change while the material remains the same
14. Compares objects that are not equal in regard to a particular property
15. Uses comparison signs (e.g., $<$, $>$)
16. Arranges objects in serial order according to a given property
17. Describes a change in an object
18. Keeps a record of observations
19. Verifies observations by repeating an activity.[15]

Personal and social development

Program Objectives

The pupil will develop peer relationships that promote social and cognitive development.

Related Student Behaviors

1. Works cooperatively with other pupils
2. Has at least one friend in class with whom to work and play
3. Can teach or explain something clearly to another pupil

Program Objectives	*Related Student Behaviors*
	4. Can receive instruction from another pupil
	5. Can express the viewpoint of another pupil in a play-acting situation, even when that viewpoint differs from his or her own.
The pupil will develop a sense of competence and mastery.	1. Completes tasks to his or her own satisfaction
	2. Shares special interests with the class
	3. Willingly undertakes new tasks
	4. Submits his/her work for display in the classroom
	5. Volunteers to help prepare new classroom materials.
The pupil will learn to assume responsibility for his or her own actions.	1. Replaces in good order the materials used
	2. Observes classroom rules
	3. Follows through on tasks he or she has volunteered for
	4. Respects the right of others in terms of a. their personal property b. their access to materials c. their right to work undisturbed.
The pupil will develop basic communication skills so as to be able to describe what has been seen, done, heard, read, etc.	1. Forms letters and writes words
	2. Writes (or dictates to an adult) stories that have a beginning, middle, and end
	3. Reads to others
	4. Enjoys being read to
	5. Listens attentively to the reading of others
	6. Follows the thoughts of others as they speak
	7. Listens to and follows the ideas in stories, discussions, etc.
	8. Listens to and follows directions
	9. Listens to messages and reports them back correctly
	10. Makes comments and adds to the subject under discussion

Program Objectives   *Related Student Behaviors*

11. Asks appropriate questions
12. Paraphrases what he or she hears
13. Participates in role-playing activities
14. Recites poems and sings songs
15. Reads and understands signs and instructions in the classroom
16. Increases his or her vocabulary
17. Consults books for information
18. Describes accurately what he or she sees
19. Describes accurately what he or she (or someone else) does.

Part 5: Checklists for Evaluating a Program Based on the Experiential Learning Model

The following two sets of checklists can be useful in evaluating the effectiveness of your program. The first checklist indicates how closely classroom procedures reflect the experential learning model; the second checklist indicates whether or not your pupils are progressing according to your expectations.

Checklist 1

How closely do classroom procedures reflect the model?

	FREQUENTLY	SOMETIMES	SELDOM
• Participation in activity is determined by pupil interest or curiosity.	☐	☐	☐
• Pupils are given opportunities to manipulate and "act on" objects or events.	☐	☐	☐
• A variety of concrete, manipulable materials are provided.	☐	☐	☐
• Materials and activities are structured so as to facilitate the development of specific thinking skills.	☐	☐	☐
• Pupils interact with others who are at differing stages of development; work with others; teach others; demonstrate and check their work with others.	☐	☐	☐
• Pupil explanations and/or questions are encouraged and valued for what they indicate about the pupil's thinking rather than for their correctness.	☐	☐	☐

Checklist 1 (continued)

	FREQUENTLY	SOMETIMES	SELDOM
• Teacher listens carefully to a pupil before reacting to what he or she says.	☐	☐	☐
• Teacher asks questions stimulating pupil observation and explanation.	☐	☐	☐
• Teacher refrains from belittling a pupil for questions or responses, and prevents others from doing the same.	☐	☐	☐

Are pupils given practice in:

	FREQUENTLY	SOMETIMES	SELDOM
• Helping to keep the classroom organized and functioning?	☐	☐	☐
• Sharing their interests with others in the classroom?	☐	☐	☐
• Receiving instruction from one another?	☐	☐	☐
• Working with one another?	☐	☐	☐
• Making choices of materials and activities?	☐	☐	☐
• Demonstrating as well as explaining the answers to questions?	☐	☐	☐
• Observing and describing (orally, in written form, or in an art medium) what they have seen or heard?	☐	☐	☐
• Checking their observations against the observations of other pupils?	☐	☐	☐
• Engaging in problem-solving activities involving number, measurement, and space?	☐	☐	☐
• Engaging in activities involving classification?	☐	☐	☐

Checklist 2

Have pupils made progress in their ability and willingness to:

	YES	UNCERTAIN	NO	or	MOST STUDENTS	SOME STUDENTS	A FEW STUDENTS
• Keep the classroom organized and functioning?	☐	☐	☐		☐	☐	☐
• Share their interests and activities with other pupils?	☐	☐	☐		☐	☐	☐

	NO	UNCERTAIN	YES		MOST STUDENTS	SOME STUDENTS	A FEW STUDENTS
• Give instruction to other pupils?	☐	☐	☐	or	☐	☐	☐
• Receive instruction from other pupils?	☐	☐	☐		☐	☐	☐
• Make choices of materials and activities?	☐	☐	☐		☐	☐	☐
• Demonstrate as well as explain answers to questions?	☐	☐	☐		☐	☐	☐
• Observe and describe what they have seen and heard?	☐	☐	☐		☐	☐	☐
• Check their observations against the observations of other pupils?	☐	☐	☐		☐	☐	☐
• Engage in problem-solving activities involving number, measurement, and space?	☐	☐	☐		☐	☐	☐
• Engage in activities involving classification?	☐	☐	☐		☐	☐	☐

Part 6: References and Resources

Athey, I. J., & Rubadeau, D. O. *Educational Implications of Piaget's Theory.* Waltham, MA: Ginn-Blaisdell, 1970.

Brearley, M. *The Teaching of Young Children: Some Applications of Piaget's Learning Theory.* New York: Schocken Books, 1972.

Charles, C. M. *Teacher's Petit Piaget.* Belmont, CA: Fearon Publishers, 1974.

Featherstone, J. *Schools Where Children Learn.* New York: Liveright, 1971.

Furth, H. *Piaget for Teachers.* Englewood Cliffs, NJ: Prentice-Hall, 1970.

Furth, H. G., & Wachs, H. *Thinking Goes to School: Piaget's Theories in Practice.* New York: Oxford University Press, 1974.

Ginsburg, H., & Opper, S. *Piaget's Theory of Intellectual Development,* 2nd ed. Englewood Cliffs, NJ: Prentice-Hall, 1979.

Goldschmid, M. L., & Bentler, P. M. *Concept Assessment Kit—Conservation.* San Diego: Educational and Industrial Testing Service, 1968.

Gorman, R. M. *Discovering Piaget: A Guide for Teachers.* Columbus, OH: Charles E. Merrill, 1972.

Joyce, B., & Weil, M. *Models of Teaching.* Englewood Cliffs, NJ: Prentice-Hall, 1972.

Lavatelli, C. *Piaget's Theory Applied to an Early Childhood Curriculum.* Boston: American Science and Engineering, 1970.

Neufeld, E. M. *The Philosophy of Jean Piaget and Its Educational Implications.* Morristown, NJ: General Learning Press, 1976.

Nuffield Foundation. *I Do and I Understand. Beginning. The Duck Pond. Apparatus. Animals and Plants, and Others.* New York: John Wiley and Sons, 1967.

Piaget, J. *Judgement and Reasoning in the Child.* London: Routledge and Kegan Paul, 1928.

Pulaski, M. A. S. *Understanding Piaget: An Introduction to Children's Cognitive Development.* San Francisco, CA: Harper & Row, 1971.

Science Curriculum Improvement Study. Boston: D. C. Heath and Company, 1967.

Sullivan, E. V. *Piaget and the School Curriculum: A Critical Appraisal.* The Ontario Institute for Studies in Education, Bulletin No. 2, 1967.

Appendix: An Introduction to the Developmental Theory of Jean Piaget

What is the nature of intelligence? How does it develop? What assists or retards its development?

Piaget defines intelligence as a process of organization and adaptation. *Organization* involves recurring psychological units of intelligent action which he calls schemas. Schemas may be thought of as types of programs or strategies that the individual uses as he or she interacts with the environment.

Adaptation is the mechanism by which the individual develops schemas for interacting with the environment. It depends upon two interdependent processes—*assimilation,* during which time the individual "takes in" environmental input and attempts to fit it into his existing intellectual patterns (schemas), and *accommodation,* during which time the individual's existing schemas are modified to deal with the new input. The schemas are repositories for past experience and therefore partial determinants of present behavior; however, they change and develop as a result of the individual's need to maintain a state of equilibrium as he interacts with his environment.

Cognitive development is characterized by a series of *equilibrium-disequilibrium* states. E. V. Sullivan explains it in this way:

In the process of assimilation the organism attempts to adapt to the environment with its already existing schemas. If assimilation is unsuccessful [if there is discrepancy between existing schemas and environmental input], a state of disequilibrium exists. Accommodation occurs as a result of this disequilibrium, and the present schemas are altered or new ones emerge.[16]

To use a simple example, grasping is a reflex schema with which the infant is born. As he or she encounters objects of different dimensions, the discovery is made that a single kind of hand movement will not suffice for all objects. Instead, the infant learns to adjust his or her hand movement to the dimensions of the object being grasped. In Piagetian terms, the infant's unsuccessful attempt to use his or her existing grasping schema is an attempt at assimilation. The failure of this attempt results in disequilibrium, which leads the infant to modify his/her grasping schema to conform to the shape of the new object. This is *accommodation:* the result is the re-establishment of equilibrium.

Figure 23 diagrams Piaget's conception of the development of intelligence through four stages. Although this diagram seems to imply that disequilibrium and reorganization occur only between stages, these are, in effect, dynamic processes which continually occur within a stage.

In this developmental process every child passes through a sequence of stages in the same order, although at different rates of speed. "The notion of 'stage' in Piaget's theory may be considered as a particular set of strategies [schemata] which are in a relative state of equilibrium at some point in the child's development."[17] The stages are hierarchical; that is, more advanced stages are dependent upon the completion of earlier stages.

The cognitive stages of development identified by Piaget and the approximate ages associated with each stage are:

1. the sensorimotor stage   0–2 years
2. the preoperational stage   2–7 years
   (preconceptual thought—until 4)
   (intuitive thought—until 7)
3. the concrete operational stage   7–11 years
4. the formal operational stage   11 years to adult

STAGE 1. SENSORIMOTOR

From infancy until approximately two years of age, the child is at the sensorimotor stage. She experiences objects directly through her five senses. Her existing organization includes the reflex schemas with which

Figure 23. The Development of Intelligence in Stages

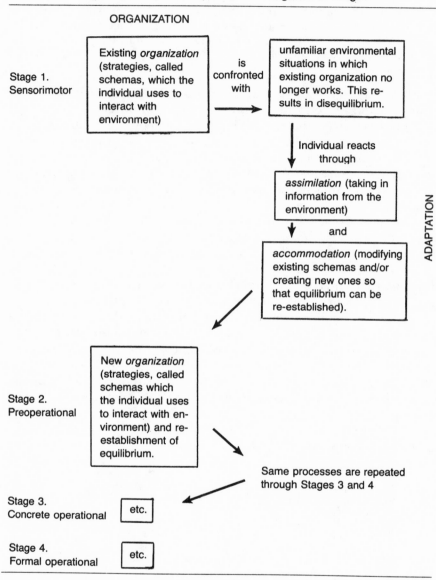

she was born. These schemas allow interaction with the surrounding world; however, the child has no schemas for internally representing or symbolizing objects. If she cannot touch, see, taste, or feel objects, they do not exist for her. Furthermore, the existing organization of the infant does not include the patterns for seeing the world as orderly, coherent, or permanent.

STAGE 2. PREOPERATIONAL

From two to approximately seven years of age, the child is at the pre-operational stage. His sensorimotor schemas continue to develop, but as a result of experience and maturation, he begins to develop new schemas for using signs and symbols—particularly words and images. Language development is the most important aspect of this stage.

Although Piaget posits that the formation of schemas of logical thought precede the verbal expression of logical thought, he maintains that language can help facilitate thought. For example, the preoperational child may be quite capable of correctly using the words "part," "whole," "more," "less," "all," and "some" in everyday situations. However, he is not able to understand class inclusion—e.g., all dogs are animals; some animals are dogs; but not all animals are dogs. When his classification operations develop enough to permit such understanding (in the concrete operational stage), the mastery of these words will be essential.

In the preoperational stage, the child is able to describe the appearance of objects even when he cannot see them. But his thought processes are still governed by his perceptions rather than by logical considerations. For example, he can attend to only a single attribute of an object at a time. After watching a small clay ball rolled into a long cylindrical shape, the child will say the long shape contains more clay than the ball. He is reaching this conclusion because he attends to the single dimension of length; he does not attach any significance to the fact that he saw no clay added to the original amount. Researchers listening to a child's explanation of events find that he considers terms such as "heavy," "big," and "full" as absolutes, inseparable from the object's identity, and that he becomes confused when a "heavy" object must be considered "light" in comparison to another object.

A child at this stage also has difficulty in making causal connections. He says that boats or cars move because "they are made that way" or because "they are alive." He explains what happens not in terms of physical causes but rather by making analogies with human behavior.

The child's thinking at this stage is egocentric, that is, tied to his own viewpoint and not challengeable by outside, contradictory evidence. He is very sure of the correctness of an answer, even if told that the answer is completely incorrect in adult terms. He does not reflect on his answer because, for him, it is the only answer possible and is therefore correct. The preoperational child is, as might be expected, incapable of taking the role or seeing the viewpoint of another person.

STAGE 3. CONCRETE OPERATIONAL

From seven until approximately eleven years of age, the child's cognitive functioning is at the concrete operational stage. In this stage, she develops the schemas that allow her to perform the following operations:

1. *Combinativity.* The child can join two classes of objects and see that she has formed a comprehensive class, e.g., the class of white wooden beads plus the class of brown wooden beads equals the class of wooden beads. The child is also able to form classes and supraclasses in hierarchical order and to comprehend that the whole is equal to the sum of its parts and is greater than any one of its parts.

2. *Reversability.* The child can reverse her thinking process. She can go back to the point at which she started to think about a problem and compare it to her current thinking about the problem. If A + B = C, then C − A = B. The child develops the intellectual organization which enables her to understand reciprocity. (That is, if A is taller than B, she knows that B must be shorter than A.) A child at the stage of concrete operations would not make the same error as this preoperational girl in answering the following questions:

Do you have a sister?   Yes

What is her name?   Ann

Does Ann have a sister?   No

3. *Associativity.* The child can combine classes knowing that the order in which they are combined is unimportant. She is able to put parts together in more than one way or think about a problem in more than one way.

4. *Identity.* The child is able to ascertain whether or not quantities are identical with one another. She is able to see that if nothing is added and nothing is taken away, an entity remains the same.

The transition between preoperational and concrete operational thinking occurs gradually and irregularly; nevertheless, there are discernible differences between stages:

In the *preoperational* stage the child, while watching water poured from a short, wide glass into a tall, slender glass, says that there is more water in the tall, slender glass, because she attends only to the single dimension of height. Later, during the *concrete operational* stage, she can attend to the relationship between height, width, and quantity all at the same time; she knows that the differences in space which the water occupies need not affect its quantity—that if one poured the water into the tall glass, it would "look" different, but the quantity of water would stay the same.

When presented with two boats that float, one large and one small, the child in the preoperational stage is likely to explain that the little boat floats because it is light, and the big boat floats because it is big (i.e., equating size with strength). She is not bothered by the fact that she has used two different "rules" to explain the same phenomenon.

As the child moves into the concrete operational stage, however, such contradictions occur in her thought process less frequently. Instead, she begins to search for logical necessities and her thought becomes flexible—that is, she can travel back in her mind to the beginning of an experiment and seek out consequences, causes, results, explanations and proofs. She can also generalize: If both heavy boats and light boats (big and little) float, then a boat's ability to float seems not to depend solely on its weight (or size).

STAGE 4. FORMAL OPERATIONAL

After eleven years of age, the child usually has the schemas to engage in formal operational thought. He can reason on the basis of verbalized theories or assumptions; he does not need direct perception and action. He can also perform all operations with language, that is, in terms of symbols.

How does the child move from stage to stage?

According to Piaget, the child's movement from stage to stage is affected by physiological maturation (which determines the range of possibilities within a stage), by interaction with the social and physical environment (which accounts for the realization of these possibilities), and by the mechanism of *equilibration*. As children proceed through each stage, they develop three classes of knowledge: logical-mathematical knowledge, social knowledge, and physical knowledge.

1. *Logical-mathematical knowledge.* Nonlogical thinking processes are gradually replaced by logical ones which enable the child to classify objects or events, to order objects or events along a particular dimension *(seriation)*, to perform operations involving number and space, and to perform operations involving temporal relationships.

2. *Social knowledge.* The child moves from egocentric and individualized ways of thinking to sociocentric and publicly validated ways of thinking in both the cognitive and social domains.

Social interaction provides a crucial ingredient for the child's cognitive development. As she interacts with peers, especially those who are a little more advanced in their development, the discrepancies between her own view of the world and theirs produces a disequilibrium that results in accommodation and the creation of new schemas.

The movement from egocentric to sociocentric is reflected in the child's use of language. Very young children when playing together engage in what Piaget calls collective monologues—that is, they talk in the company of other children, but without expecting the other children to listen or respond. Socialized speech, on the other hand, is communicative in its intention.

The movement from egocentric to sociocentric is also reflected in the child's perspective. In the preoperational stage, the young child can neither describe the visual perspective of another person, nor comprehend the emotional perspective of another person. It is quite useless, therefore, to say to a three- or four-year-old, "How would you feel if Johnny did that to you?"

As the child moves into the concrete operational stage, however, she begins to be able to differentiate, socially as well as cognitively, her own perspective from that of others. Previously, the child judged an act solely by its consequence; now she begins to consider the intention of an act. She also begins to see rules as important social conventions that are subject to change, rather than as absolute, unchangeable entities. This is the time, too, when a child begins to acquire socially defined concepts, such as "honesty," "bravery," etc.

3. *Physical knowledge.* As the child moves from sensorimotor to preoperational and operational thought, she develops schemas of object permanence. She comes to know the regularity of an object's behavior; she becomes able to predict the results of a given act on a given object; she comes to know that the physical world has regularity. The child learns all this by acting on objects and observing and systematizing the results of these actions.

7
The Group
Inquiry Model

Group inquiry teaches children how to acquire and organize information while participating as members of a small group. The model[1] is based on the assumption that children who engage in group problem-solving activities will learn useful social skills as well as an effective method for dealing with a wide variety of subjects.

Introduction

PART 1. A Classroom Example

PART 2. Procedures for Using the Group Inquiry Model in the Classroom

PART 3. Settings Needed When Using the Group Inquiry Model

PART 4. Anticipated Student Outcomes of Using the Group Inquiry Model

PART 5. Checklists for Evaluating a Program Based on the Group Inquiry Model

PART 6. References and Resources

Introduction

The group inquiry model is derived from the work of two groups of educational investigators: Herbert Thelen and others from the University of Chicago, who stress the educational potential of group processes;[2] and Lippitt, Fox, and Schaible from the University of Michigan, who stress the educational potential of social science research methods.[3]

Thelen feels that pupils should be helped to inquire into any situations they have questions about. He further believes that this inquiry should be conducted in small groups so that the pupils may learn not only about the subject matter, but also about learning in a cooperative manner. Thelen's overall plan for group inquiry is to present situations that are likely to evoke varied reactions from children. The latter then identify questions they want to investigate, consider what is required to carry out the investigation, learn investigative techniques, do the investigating and, finally, report and evaluate the results.[4]

Lippitt suggests that pupils should process information by using the methods of the research scientist. He believes that this experience will teach them that knowledge is gained by collecting, analyzing, combining, and generalizing from bits and pieces of information or data.

The group inquiry model calls both for group processes and for inquiry processes as summarized in Figure 24.

Assumptions of the group inquiry model

1. The "facts" of a discipline are better understood by pupils if they take part in the process of "discovering" them.
2. The natural curiosity of children will motivate them to seek solutions to problems that interest them.

Figure 24. Processes Involved in Group Inquiry[5]

Group Processes	Inquiry Processes
1. sharing ideas and perceptions	1. formulating important questions and/or generating hypotheses
2. forming groups, then deciding on and assigning jobs	2. deciding what information is needed to answer questions, and how to obtain it
3. communicating, resolving conflicts, sharing responsibilities, being leader, recorder, and summarizer	3. collecting and recording information
4. deciding on and preparing ways of communicating the group's findings	4. analyzing information, drawing conclusions, and making generalizations
5. evaluating group processes including roles, communications, etc.	5. reformulating questions in light of new discoveries, and discussing the strong and weak points of the investigation.

3. Participating in group problem-solving activities will help them clarify their ideas by discussing them with their peers.
4. Participating in group problem-solving activities will also help them learn the social skills necessary for working effectively with others.
5. Children can and should learn the processes of systematic inquiry.

Part 1: A Classroom Example

Ms. Johnson, a seventh-grade teacher, heard about the group inquiry model and decided to use it in her science class. To start the group inquiry

---
Introduce a general topic.

---

process, she decided she would first introduce a general topic, and then let the interests of the students guide the direction of the inquiry. With this in mind, she showed the class a film on insects—a film which had generated considerable student interest in her previous class. The comments of her pupils subsequent to the film indicated that they had enjoyed it.

Ms. Johnson began the discussion which followed by asking her class, "What do you think of when I say the word 'insect'?"

"I think of snails," Mary Jane said. "My dad is always worried about the snails eating his favorite flowers."

"A snail isn't an insect, is it?" Robert interrupted.

"Let's look at some pictures of insects and see," Ms. Johnson suggested.

Present the situation and formulate the questions.

She then displayed a number of large posters with pictures of various kinds of insects. She told the class a little about the general characteristics of insects, but her real intention was to lead the class to ask questions about the insects and then have the children do research to find the answers.

To get them started, Ms. Johnson said, "Some people think we should try to do away with insects. Do you agree?"

"Yeah, man!" Erica said. "I hate insects. I'd like to wipe them out!"

Mary Jane heatedly replied, "No! Insects are useful."

"No, they aren't," said Erica. "I read about insects. They cause disease. And my mom is always throwing out food because of the bugs."

"My lizard wouldn't like it if there weren't any insects. There wouldn't be anything for him to eat," Jim offered.

"What about chocolate-covered ants? I'll bet you eat those!" Ralph countered.

"Actually, I've heard that some people in other countries eat insects. Is that true?" John asked. "Eating bugs might not be a bad idea, especially if people are starving."

Ms. Johnson interrupted the laughter which followed John's comments. "We have at least two different kinds of feelings here, it seems. A few of you want to eliminate insects; others think they are useful—maybe even as a possible food source for people."

Soon the class began to ask other questions. Several pupils were clearly interested in the edibility of insects. Some seemed interested to learn how insects could help or harm man. Still others wanted to know how insects fly (they were also interested in how birds and airplanes fly). Teresa inquired about insect families and wanted to know if all insects live in families or if just bees and ants do.

Ms. Johnson helped the class organize its questions into separate areas of investigation. Five categories emerged:

1. Are insects a possible food source? If so, how could people be persuaded to eat them?
2. In what ways are insects harmful to people? In what ways do they help people?
3. Do insects make good pets?
4. How do insects fly? Do they fly in the same way that birds or airplanes fly?
5. Do insects have families? If so, how do they live?

Ms. Johnson decided with the help of the class that each category would provide the basis for a group investigation, and that each pupil would choose the group he/she wished to join.

Before the class began to meet in groups, however, Ms. Johnson felt that the children could use guidance in group processes. So she planned some lessons, one of which was organized around a filmstrip dealing with the idea of working cooperatively in groups. The filmstrip covered several techniques for expressing ideas, listening, and coming to a group consensus.

She then had pupils role-play a hypothetical situation based on the filmstrip in which half of a group wanted to present a play, whereas the other half wished to prepare a bulletin board display. The class enjoyed this role-playing activity and decided that, if a particular group ran into difficulties, it could call the whole class together to discuss and role-play ways of solving the problem(s).

Plan the investigation.

In the days that followed, the various groups met in different corners of the room and discussed what they specifically wanted to find out, and how. They also talked about what kinds of jobs would have to be done, and who would do each job.

Conduct the investigation.

For example, Group 1 (the group investigating the edibility of insects) made the chart illustrated in Figure 25, with Ms. Johnson's help. As Group 1 worked out its plan, its members felt that it would also be fun to try an advertising campaign. The goal of this campaign would be to get pupils in other classes to react favorably to the idea of eating insects.

Figure 25. An Investigative Plan

Question: Are insects a possible food source? If so, how can people be persuaded to eat them?

What information do we want?	What resources might be helpful?	Job description	Job assignment
Are insects poisonous? Are insects nutritious?	Poison Center Library books Dietitian Dept. of Entomology at university	Prepare and conduct interviews with poison center staff, dietitian, entomologist	Bob & Linda
Are there people who eat insects? What kind of insects? Are they palatable?	Library research Anthropology Dept. at university Food and Drug Administration	Do library research Prepare and conduct interviews with anthropologist Write letter to FDA	Anna, Mark, & Karen Anna
How plentiful are insects for food purposes? Would it be difficult to raise or catch them?	Dept. of Entomology Dept. of Agriculture Farmers' Almanac and other library resources	Prepare and conduct interviews Do library research	Carol Ted

Noting that some children were planning to collect information through the use of interviews and questionnaires, Ms. Johnson called in a social science researcher who explained to the class how to construct questionnaires and how to conduct interviews.

It wasn't long before Ms. Johnson noted that Group 3 (which was investigating the question, "Do insects make good pets?") was not working well together. After some thought, she concluded that there was not sufficient interest in the topic, and so she asked the pupils to join another group.

Present the findings.

The children were now ready to present their findings to one another. The group exploring the edibility of insects had prepared an "insect information center" which consisted of visual displays and written reports on the questions they had researched. The group's presentation to the class involved explaining how individual students could use the center as well as presenting a TV advertisement about insects as nutritious food.

The group that had investigated the question whether insects are helpful or harmful to people presented its information orally. It used a debate format: "Resolved: That insects do more harm than good to man."

The group that had addressed the question of how insects fly prepared a chart and a model of a flying insect to use in its oral presentation to the class.

The group that had been gathering information on insect families wrote and illustrated a book on this subject. Included were some stories and poems which Ms. Johnson later read to the entire class.

Evaluate the investigation.

Finally, the students helped Ms. Johnson design a questionnaire to evaluate group processes. This questionnaire is shown in Figure 26. Everyone in the class answered the questions; then Ms. Johnson tallied the results and discussed them in turn with each group and with the entire class.

Part 2: Procedures for Using the Group Inquiry Model in the Classroom[6]

In sequencing activities in a group inquiry process, it is important to remain flexible and take your cues from your pupils. As you know,

Figure 26. A Group Process Questionnaire

Name _____   Group _____

1. What job(s) did you do? _____

_____

_____

_____

	Yes	Not Sure	No
2. Did you do your job well?	____	____	____
3. Did your group work well together?	____	____	____
4. Did the group think of good questions?	____	____	____
5. Were you pleased with your group's final presentation?	____	____	____
6. Did you enjoy working in your group?	____	____	____

Comments* _____

_____

_____

_____

*Should include information about what they felt they had learned, and how they might do things differently on the next project.

children react and learn at different rates of speed and in different ways. Therefore, you may have to reteach certain steps, or move quickly through others. Figure 27 presents the five steps in using group inquiry.

Figure 27. Steps in Using Group Inquiry

1. Present the situation and formulate the inquiry questions.

2. Plan the investigation.

3. Conduct the investigation.

4. Present the findings.

5. Evaluate the investigation.

1. Present the situation and formulate the inquiry questions.

One of your first tasks will be to create a classroom atmosphere in which pupils can present their ideas to their peers and be assured their ideas will be treated with respect. Your pupils may need special instruction and practice in sharing ideas and perceptions in a courteous, orderly fashion. One way of providing such instruction and practice is to design special activities for that purpose prior to the group activities. Another way is to work with them in their groups as they conduct their inquiry.

Once this has been done, you can present an interesting or puzzling situation to them in the form of a story, film, description, or demonstration. Include one or two questions to stimulate their interest, but be careful not to ask too many questions. (Remember, that will be the job of the children.)

A situation suitable for stimulating inquiry has three characteristics: It is puzzling, intriguing, or meaningful to the children; it is appropriate to the intellectual level of the children; and it is general enough so that they will ask many questions about it.

Help your pupils to formulate answerable questions about any given situation. To do this, make sure they are able to discriminate between a question which is appropriate for investigation and one which is not. A question that can be answered by investigation is *one for which evidence can be gathered.*[7] For example:

- What are some of the ways in which Hemingway's protagonists are alike?
- How serious is the problem of dental cavities in our community?
- How do insects transmit disease?

Another type of question that can be answered by investigation is *one which implies the kind of information needed.* For instance: Which prehistoric animals resembled animals of today? How did Gauguin's techniques revolutionize the style of painting accepted in his time? What physical pheonomena in wave production (wavelength, oscillation, etc.) account for the dimensions of sound (pitch, volume, etc.)?

If a question is so general that it covers the entire spectrum of a topic, it will clearly be difficult to decide what information is needed to answer it. For example: What do we know about dinosaurs? How does art reflect history? What components of sound account for what we hear? On the other hand, a question worth investigating is *one which requires more than an obvious or trivial answer.* In other words, the question must not be so specific that little or no inquiry will be necessary to answer it. For instance:

• Who won the battle of Gettysburg?

• Is a rhinoceros an herbivore or a carnivore?

With practice, pupils can learn to phrase questions in a way that will guide them to systematic, cooperative investigation.

Three alternative procedures you can use to help your pupils think critically about the kinds of questions they are asking are as follows:

• Choose a subject; then encourage the pupils to ask as many questions as they wish about the subject. Discuss each question, applying the aforementioned criteria, and decide whether or not the question is answerable by investigation and, if so, whether it is *worth* investigating.

• Compile a list of questions. Discuss each in terms of the kinds of information which it may lead to.

• Ask questions about the pupils' questions. For example, if a student asks, "What can we find out about dinosaurs?" you in turn can ask: "What exactly do you want to find out about dinosaurs? What categories of information could you investigate?"

The list of question types appearing in Figure 28 can be used to help pupils generate "investigative" questions.

2. Plan the investigation.

Before beginning an investigation with the children, remember that you want to encourage them to make their *own* decisions. So always give your pupils the time and opportunity to generate suggestions and ideas.

There are a number of skills that pupils should have in order to know how to plan an investigation effectively. You may want to introduce some of these skills to the entire class prior to or during the investigation itself. Or, you may want to work on the development of these skills with one group at a time. For example, everyone may need help in thinking of the appropriate methods for summarizing and displaying the findings of an investigation. In such a case, you would want to instruct the class as a whole. On the other hand, if one group is having difficulty in formulating topics, you may want to work with that group alone, permitting the others to continue to work independently.

Your pupils may need help with any or all of the following tasks:

• Organizing inquiry groups in such a way that each group has the responsibility for investigating a major question

• Listing the subtopics for each question to be investigated

• Discussing the resources needed to obtain information about each question

Figure 28. Questions for Group Inquiry[8]

Question Types

---

1. **Descriptive:** What happened? What are they doing? What is going on? How many different kinds are there?

2. **Comparative:** How are they different from each other? How are they similar? How would scientists do it?

3. **Historical:** When and how did it start? Has it changed from the way it used to be? What has been found to be true in the past?

4. **Conceptual:** Why would you group these things together? What belongs together? What name would you give this group?

5. **Causal:** Why did it turn out this way? What caused it to act in this manner?

6. **Relational:** How is this event related to that event? Why did you think of this other event?

7. **Predictive:** How will it end? What do you think will happen next?

8. **Hypothetical:** If we do this, what will happen? If this, then what?

9. **Methodological:** How did we find that out? Where can we locate resources? Are our observations reliable? How valid are our data?

10. **Value-Oriented:** Which way do you think is best? Is it always bad to do it this way?

11. **Relevant:** How does this apply to us? How does this apply to similar situations?

12. **Definitional:** What do we mean by this term? What characteristics would identify our examples? How could we define what we mean so that everyone will agree with our definition?

- Deciding on how to present the results of the investigation to the class
- Assigning jobs for which individuals will be responsible.

1. *Organize inquiry groups.*[9] An inquiry group should be small enough so that each individual can be heard, can have a contributing role, and can become well acquainted with the other members of the group. If possible, the group should include students of diverse talents, opinions, backgrounds, and skills. Such diversity will enrich the learning experience by exposing students to perspectives different from their own. Don't hesitate to experiment with alternative kinds of groupings to discover which kind works best for your pupils.

Here are two possible ways to group the class:

• Let the pupils decide which groups they want to belong to. This decision should be based either on their interest in the questions or on their wish to work with particular peers.

• Form groups based on the kind of "mix" you want. You may assign pupils to each group based on your knowledge of their abilities, talents, interests, friendships, needs, etc.

Before forming the groups, consider what should be done with the dominating personalities in the class, as well as with immature pupils and isolates. Unfortunately, there is no "best" way to make these decisions. But the more you use group techniques, the more skillful you will become at helping pupils to form productive groups.[10]

2. *List the subtopics for each question to be investigated.* Once the inquiry groups are formed, you should help the children to break down the original questions into more specific topics. Doing this will direct the pupils to appropriate resources and research areas.

Provide time for the children to "think" about their questions. Suggest that they look through encyclopedias, textbooks, atlases, magazines, or other reference sources to explore the full range of their topic.

3. *Discuss the resources needed to obtain information.* Encourage pupils to think about all the possible places they may find information. (A list of such resources is presented in Figure 29, which is organized according to four classifications: people, institutions, media, and personal experience.)

4. *Decide on how to present the results of the investigation.* After all the inquiry groups have decided on their topics and the resources they will use to explore them, they should discuss among themselves how they will tell others about what they have discovered. (A list of possible final presentations is provided in Figure 30.)

Although deciding at this time on the form the final presentation will take may seem premature, there are several reasons why it should be discussed during planning procedures:

• The form of the final product may determine how the group collects and organizes its information.
• The pupils may need time to learn how to "create" their presentation, and time should definitely be made available for this purpose.
• Making a presentation requires much work involving many different kinds of tasks. While some of this work can be done concurrently with the work of the actual investigation, other parts of it may well have to be scheduled earlier.

Figure 29. Resources

People

experts in the field   heads of organizations
teachers   heads of special agencies
practitioners in the field   school personnel, etc.
neighbors and community people

Institutions

private businesses involved in manufacturing, services, retailing of products
societies formed for specific purposes (e.g., Audubon Society, Sierra Club, etc.)
government agencies (e.g., FCC, FDA, Postal Service, etc.)
schools
research institutions (e.g., Salk Institute, research hospitals, etc.)

Media

Printed	*Mass Media*	*Audiovisual*
trade books	magazines	tapes
textbooks	newspapers	films
encyclopedias	television	filmstrips
dictionaries	radio	records
journal articles	movies	video cassettes
historical documents		
letters		
almanacs		
non-fiction		
fiction		

Personal Experience

experiments   thinking
observations   introspection

---

5. *Assign the jobs that individuals will be responsible for.* There are basically three types of jobs that must be assigned:

a. *Jobs related to the investigation.* These can be formulated by working from the list of suggested topics and/or the list of suggested resources. The pupils in each group should suggest and describe what investigative jobs they feel are necessary. Such jobs might include:

• using reference books (atlases, encyclopedias, almanacs, etc.)
• interpreting an experiment

Figure 30. Final Presentations

Written

autobiography	dictionary	notebook
biography	letter	outline
book report	list	report
booklet	newspaper	story

Oral

debate	experiment	song
demonstration	interview	speech
discussion	oral report	story telling

Dramatic

dramatization	play	skit
pantomime	puppet show	

Graphic

calendar	graph	poster
cartoon	map	puzzle
chart	mural	scrapbook
construction	painting	scroll
diorama	picture dictionary	time line

- conducting an experiment
- obtaining the equipment or supplies for an experiment
- writing a questionnaire
- using a questionnaire
- interviewing people in person or on the phone
- compiling lists
- observing other people
- writing letters
- taking notes on lectures, films, television programs, etc.
- outlining.

Many of the jobs suggested above require a certain level of knowledge or skill. Figure 31 is a checklist of investigative skills that your pupils should ideally have.

b. *Jobs related to the final presentation.* You and your pupils can anticipate the requirements of this project by asking yourselves the following questions:

- What materials will be needed?
- What special equipment will be required?

Figure 31. Investigative Skills

Checklist

	Yes	No
People		
Do the pupils know how to request an interview?	___	___
Are they able to ask questions and write down the answers concurrently?	___	___
Are they able to devise questionnaires and ask people to complete them?	___	___
Do they know telephone etiquette?	___	___
Are they able to write a letter requesting information?	___	___
Institutions		
Are the pupils able to find the name of the institution which might deal with what they are interested in?	___	___
Do they know how to find out about an agency's policy on disseminating information?	___	___
Do they know how to contact a particular person or department within an institution?	___	___
Media		
Do the pupils know how to use the library's card catalogue?	___	___
Do they know how to find a particular book in the library?	___	___
Do they know how to locate magazine articles?	___	___
Do they know where audiovisual materials can be found?	___	___
Do they know how to use a table of contents and an index?	___	___
Do they know how to use an encyclopedia? Its index?	___	___
Do they know how to use the telephone book?	___	___
Personal Experience		
Do the pupils know how to use a ruler?	___	___
Do they know how to use a microscope? Binoculars?	___	___
Can they follow an experimental procedure?	___	___
Can they follow an observation plan?	___	___
Can they answer a self-report questionnaire?	___	___

- What kind of communication skills (speaking, writing) should the group have? What artistic and technical skills? What social interaction skills?
- How much time will be needed to complete this project satisfactorily?

c. *Jobs related to group processes.* Within each group, there is bound to be much interaction. Ideas will be offered, decisions will have to be made, and compromises will almost certainly be necessary. You may feel, therefore, that the groups will run more smoothly if certain "group process jobs" are initially assigned. You may also feel that learning about and practicing these group maintenance functions are important educational goals.

Three group process jobs that your pupils should be able to handle, if given some instruction, are:

- leader
- recorder
- summarizer

3. Conduct the investigation.

Although the actual work of the investigation is done by the children themselves, you have a major "behind the scenes" job seeing to it that each group functions efficiently and follows through logically with its work.[11] You must monitor each project, help the pupils work together, be sensitive to any problems that arise, and attend to them before they become serious.

In checking to make sure that each group is "on target," ask yourself the following questions:

Is the group successful in reaching decisions and carrying them out?

- Does each member of the group participate in the decision-making process?
- Do the members of the group compromise?
- Does the group follow through on decisions?
- Are the members accomplishing what they set out to do?
- Is the project moving along?

Are pupils functioning with confidence and independence as group members?

- Does the group get started on its own?
- Does the group work without bothering the others?
- Does the group stick to tasks that are relevant to its investigation?

Are pupils motivated and involved with what they are doing?

• Does the group seem busy, enthusiastic, happy?
• Does the group show initiative, momentum?
• Does the group have a sense of purpose?

Are there harmonious working relations within the group?

• Is there a minimum of fighting and belittling comments?
• Does the group resolve its differences through constructive arguments and discussion?
• Is the atmosphere in the group friendly, easy, and relaxed?
• Do the pupils listen to one another?
• Do the pupils feel that each member in the group has contributed to the group's overall accomplishments?

Summary. It is important that you be available, if necessary, to assist the pupils in performing the varied jobs required in conducting their investigation, making their presentation, and maintaining group harmony. To achieve all this, you should function as liaison person, resource person, counselor, and consultant. Be prepared to provide assistance in any or all of the following situations:

• Sometimes pupils need instruction in how to perform certain tasks. Help them to develop whatever skills they lack.
• Sometimes they need special materials and equipment. Show them how and where to obtain them.
• Sometimes they need help in contacting resource persons. Assist them.
• Sometimes they need to know how to organize their time so that the work gets done efficiently. Teach them how to allocate their time and use it properly.
• Sometimes they need help in resolving interpersonal problems. Show them how to negotiate and effect compromises. Teach them how to express their opinions tactfully, without injuring the feelings of others, and how to listen to and make use of the opinions of others.

4. Present the findings.

After each group has finished its investigation, the students will then share their findings (via the final presentation) with an audience—other members of their class, the rest of the school, their parents, City Hall, etc.

Having a group present the results of its investigation serves several purposes. It allows the members of that group to summarize information, interpret it, draw conclusions, and explain the reasons for their conclusions. It also allows them to be creative (by sharing their investigation in the form of a play, diorama, newspaper, cartoon, mural, etc.) and to discover new competencies and areas of interest. In short, children who previously "blended into the background" may "blossom" and gain real pride in their joint or individual accomplishments.

5. Evaluate the investigation.

Up to this point, the pupils have been involved in many different activities. They have:

- confronted a problem
- formulated questions
- planned an investigation by deciding on informational needs, resources, form of final presentation, etc.
- conducted an investigation
- presented findings.

The children have also worked within a group, in which they have:

- shared different perceptions and reactions
- made group decisions
- assumed a variety of responsibilities
- carried out and followed through on jobs individually or together
- worked together to present the group's work via a final presentation.

Remember: Even after the investigation has been completed, the children can still learn from their experience. They have been "learning by doing"; now it is time for them to "learn by reflecting on" what has just occurred. In other words, the activities and steps of the inquiry process become the subject for discussion. Although these discussions can take place throughout the investigation, they should constitute the final activity of group inquiry.

In evaluting the group inquiry process, the pupils should focus on the following areas:

1. *The questions that directed the inquiry*
   - Were the questions important?
   - Were they interesting?

2. *The conduct of the investigation*
   • What did they learn from the experience?
   • How would they do things differently next time?

3. *The group processes*
   • Did they enjoy the group experience?
   • Did they enjoy the planning?
   • Did they enjoy their responsibilities?
   • What (if anything) hampered their progress as a group?

In addition to discussion, you may wish to obtain the reactions of the pupils in other ways. Some of the possibilities available to you are suggested in Figure 32.

Part 3: Settings Needed When Using the Group Inquiry Model

Materials

The effectiveness and success of group inquiry will depend in part on the availability of materials—materials for you, resources for the pupils. As far as you yourself are concerned, try to explore areas for possible investigation by your pupils. Your explorations may take you to libraries, book stores, media centers, and/or publishers' catalogues. In terms of students' resources, you may use or adapt adult-level reading material, obtain the assistance of parents or aides, and/or use non-textual sources (speakers, films, tapes, etc.). The first or second time you use the group inquiry model in your class, you are likely to be hampered by a lack of materials. However, as you become more experienced, you will develop a growing number of resources. You will also be able to use the reports, displays, and products of previous classes as resource materials for the current inquiry.

Consider not only the materials themselves but how to facilitate their use. In this connection, you may allow some pupils to work in the school library or media center. You may encourage others to use the public library—perhaps by sending letters home to their parents describing the project and emphasizing the desirability of their children's library work. Within the classroom, you will want to decide whether encyclopedias, books, or magazines may be borrowed for home use, if they should be

Figure 32. Sample Formats for Evaluating Group Inquiry Experiences[12]

---

1. Write an essay evaluating your group's experiences. Cover such topics as:
   • what your group did well
   • what your group *did not* do well, and how you think these shortcomings might be overcome in future group inquiry experiences
   • what you, personally, gained from the group inquiry experience.

2. How do you feel about your own contribution to the group?

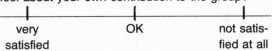

| very | OK | not satis- |
| satisfied | | fied at all |

How do you feel about the way your group worked as a team?

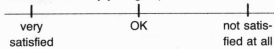

| very | OK | not satis- |
| satisfied | | fied at all |

How do you feel about the results of your team's work?

| very | OK | not satis- |
| satisfied | | fied at all |

	Most of the Time	*Some of the Time*	*Rarely*
3. Check the following:			
• Members of our group were friendly and helpful to one another.	____	____	____
• Our group was able to get the information we needed.	____	____	____
• Everyone in our group did his/her share of the work.	____	____	____
• Members of our group were satisfied with the jobs they were assigned.	____	____	____

---

used anywhere within the classroom, or if they should be restricted to a particular corner of the room. Similarly, you may wish to establish rules governing the marking or cutting up of materials, and to develop a checkout system to keep resources from disappearing.

The storage of materials is a related consideration. Set up, or help the pupils set up, a filing system for materials—either on open shelves, in labeled boxes, in a cupboard, or on a special table. Since you probably want to make it possible for them to work with a minimum amount of direction, create a storage system that will make it easy for pupils to find and replace materials.

Classroom organization

Different organizational patterns will occur within the classroom at each stage of the inquiry process. At times you will be working with the entire class; at other intervals, the pupils may be working in small groups; and, then again, each member of the group may be pursuing his or her own private investigation.

There are many ways in which you can arrange the classroom so that pupils can work effectively in groups. Here are some examples:

• Ms. Smith has four inquiry groups, each working in one of the corners of her classroom. A group of students in the middle of the room is doing individual work at their seats. Ms. Smith walks around the room, visiting the various groups in turn.

• A group of seven pupils from Ms. Ellis's class is meeting in the library with the librarian in order to learn library skills. In the meantime, Ms. Ellis and the rest of the class are having a classroom lesson unrelated to the group inquiry topics.

• Everyone in Ms. Joplin's class is a member of a group. Once each week, each group chooses a time and place to meet *outside* of the classroom—at a home, in another room after school, during lunch in the cafeteria, etc. Ms. Joplin tries to meet with each group at least once a week.

• Each table in Mr. Lee's class seats a group. Every day, when the pupils finish their assigned work, they have a quiet meeting at their seats. Mr. Lee checks on each group's meeting.

• Mr. Matthew's class is divided into five inquiry groups. Most of these groups are busy producing their final presentation. The classroom is a bustle of purposeful activity. Some of the furniture has been temporarily moved so that Group X can paint its mural and draw its graphs, while Group Z can set up its health-food convenience mart.

Personnel

As you might infer from the above descriptions of classroom organization, it is possible for your pupils to work in groups even if you do not have additional adult assistance. Such classroom assistance does help, however. Teacher aides, tutors from upper grades, volunteer parents, and student teachers are all possible sources of such assistance.

If you do enlist the participation of aides, define their responsibilities clearly. They should be aware, for example, that the pupils are supposed to be planning and conducting the investigation, while you are teaching them the prerequisite skills. In other words, other adults or older students should only be facilitators and helpers; they should *not* take over either the pupils' investigations or your own teaching responsibilities.

Schedule

Depending on the subject area, the five steps in group inquiry should be so set up as to comprise a complete unit of study. If you know the amount of time you wish to devote to the entire unit, you can allocate the proportionate time for each activity. The amount of time required for each of the steps may vary considerably, depending on the skill levels of the children and on the complexity and difficulty of their investigation. You can find an example of the way time may be allocated in Figure 33.

Figure 33. Sample Schedule for Ten-Week Group Inquiry Project

Time	Step
Week 1	Present the situation and formulate the questions
Week 2	Plan the investigation
Weeks 3–7	Conduct the investigation
Weeks 8–9	Present the findings
Week 10	Evaluate the investigation

Part 4: Anticipated Student Outcomes of Using the Group Inquiry Model

This section provides a list of skills that children may acquire from participating in a program based on the group inquiry model. The list is by no means exhaustive, so add to it and/or adapt it to the specific needs of your pupils.

The student outcomes listed below are written at two levels of specificity: Program objectives appearing in the left-hand column are general; related behaviors will be found in the right-hand column.*

Program Objectives	*Related Student Behaviors*
The pupil will develop the ability and willingness to articulate a viewpoint.	1. After hearing a number of different viewpoints, will select the viewpoint that most closely matches his or her own 2. Will not hesitate to express his or her opinion even if it differs from the opinion held by the group 3. Will share his or her thoughts and feelings 4. Will express positive feelings about asking questions.
The pupil will identify questions amenable to investigation and seek answers to these questions.	1. Given a description of a situation or event, will indicate the aspect of the situation or event that interests or puzzles him or her 2. Given an interesting or puzzling situation, will ask a number of relevant questions 3. Given a problem, will express positive feelings to the teacher about discovering the answers him or herself.
The pupil will participate actively and effectively in a working group.	1. After an initial meeting with a group, will identify the purpose of that group 2. Will name the functions of leader, secretary, summarizer of group discussions 3. Will be able to perform the functions of leader, secretary, summarizer of group discussions 4. Given a small-group discussion, will contribute at least _____ percent of the time 5. Given a small-group discussion, will make comments relevant to the discussion

*All outcomes should be rewritten in terms of your particular subject area.

Program Objectives	*Related Student Behaviors*

6. Given a group discussion where two opposing viewpoints are expressed, will suggest possible compromises
7. Will listen to viewpoints that differ from his or her own
8. Will express willingness to consider seriously viewpoints that differ from his or her own
9. Will express views so that others understand or identify his or her position
10. Will not physically or verbally attack another person in the group
11. Will be able to identify different viewpoints expressed during a group discussion
12. Will perform tasks which further the group's purposes
13. Will express pleasure at the prospect of participating in a group experience
14. Given a decision arrived at through compromise or consensus, will follow through on this decision even if it conflicts with his or her own position.

The pupil will be able to plan an investigation.

1. Given a general question, will suggest subtopics that focus on the information needed
2. Given a broad question and a list of topics, will identify those topics that directly relate to the question
3. Given the names of resource materials, will identify the places where they can be found or the persons who can dispense them
4. Given a topic to investigate, will suggest resources which could provide useful information, and tell where these resources might be located
5. Given a topic to investigate, will select those resources which provide basic information about the topic

Program Objectives	*Related Student Behaviors*
	6. Given a topic of interest and a resource he or she has used before, will explain how to use the resource in order to find relevant information about the topic
	7. Given a list of topics and appropriate resources, will name the research job he or she prefers
	8. Given a number of research jobs to be completed by the group, will be able to suggest equitable allocations of time and responsibility
	9. Given a number of research jobs to be completed by the group, will contribute to a discussion in which these responsibilities are allocated
	10. Given a topic and a list of "final presentations," will select those presentations most appropriate to the topic
	11. Given a list of final presentations, will select those he or she prefers to make or do
	12. Given a list of research jobs for his or her group, will estimate the amount of time it will take to do these jobs
	13. Given a final presentation idea for his or her group, will estimate the amount of time necessary to produce it
	14. Given a task for which several skills are required, will identify the skills he or she does or does not have
	15. Given a research or production task, will list the jobs that must be done in order to complete the task.
The pupil will carry out an investigative plan.	1. Given a task, will follow through on this task, seeking help only when he or she needs it
	2. Will persist with a task until it is completed
	3. Given a description of a data-collection method, will collect the information as prescribed

Program Objectives	*Related Student Behaviors*
	4. Given a choice of data-collection methods, will identify the one that is most useful for his or her purpose
	5. Given a project requiring input from more than one person, will work with others to complete the project.
The pupil will present a written, oral, and/or graphic representation of the results of the investigation.	1. Will summarize, if required to do so, the information he or she has gathered
	2. Will draw conclusions from his or her summarized information
	3. Will be able to describe a. the answer(s) or partial answer(s) to the question investigated b. the methods used to obtain the information c. some conclusions, generalizations, or questions that resulted from the investigation.
The pupil will evaluate an investigation he/she has participated in.	1. Will express a willingness to evaluate his or her own work
	2. Will offer constructive criticism of his or her work, as well as the work of others in the group
	3. After investigation is completed, will indicate specific strengths and weaknesses of that investigation.

Part 5: Checklists for Evaluating a Program Based on the Group Inquiry Model

The following two sets of checklists can be useful in evaluating the effectiveness of your program. The first checklist indicates how closely classroom procedures reflect the group inquiry model; the second checklist indicates whether or not your pupils are progressing according to your expectations.

Checklist 1

How closely do classroom procedures reflect the model?

	FREQUENTLY	SOMETIMES	SELDOM
• Pupils are presented with situations which are interesting or puzzling to them for the purpose of formulating questions for group inquiry.	☐	☐	☐
• Pupils have access to various resources that are at an appropriate level of difficulty for their investigations.	☐	☐	☐
• Pupils work in a group of a size and composition that permits each member to contribute.	☐	☐	☐
• Pupils are given opportunities to play different roles within their groups.	☐	☐	☐
• Pupils are permitted to conduct their own groups and to make most decisions with a minimum of interference.	☐	☐	☐
• Teacher monitors projects and sees to it that pupils work harmoniously and purposefully.	☐	☐	☐

Are pupils given practice in:

• Generating inquiry questions?	☐	☐	☐
• Distinguishing among types of questions and identifying those which are amenable to investigation?	☐	☐	☐
• Listening to the views of others and articulating their own views?	☐	☐	☐
• Considering a number of potential resources that can provide information for their investigations and selecting from among these resources?	☐	☐	☐
• Using a variety of resources?	☐	☐	☐
• Participating in the planning of a group investigation?	☐	☐	☐
• Assuming responsibility for carrying out portions of the plan?	☐	☐	☐
• Presenting written, oral, and/or graphic representations of the results of the investigation?	☐	☐	☐
• Participating in the evaluation of the processes and products of the group investigation?	☐	☐	☐

Checklist 2

Have pupils made progress in their ability and willingness to:

	YES	UNCERTAIN	NO		MOST STUDENTS	SOME STUDENTS	A FEW STUDENTS
• Generate questions?	☐	☐	☐	or	☐	☐	☐

	YES	UNCERTAIN	NO		MOST STUDENTS	SOME STUDENTS	A FEW STUDENTS
• Distinguish among types of questions and identify those which are amenable to investigation?	☐	☐	☐ or		☐	☐	☐
• Listen to the views of others and articulate their own views?	☐	☐	☐		☐	☐	☐
• Consider a number of potential resources that can provide the information for their investigations and select from among these resources?	☐	☐	☐		☐	☐	☐
• Use a variety of resources?	☐	☐	☐		☐	☐	☐
• Participate in the planning of a group investigation?	☐	☐	☐		☐	☐	☐
• Assume responsibility for carrying out portions of the plan?	☐	☐	☐		☐	☐	☐
• Present written, oral, and/or graphic representations of the results of the investigation?	☐	☐	☐		☐	☐	☐
• Participate in the evaluation of the processes and products of the group investigation?	☐	☐	☐		☐	☐	☐

Part 6: References and Resources

Flynn, E. W., & La Faso, J. F. *Group Discussion as a Learning Process: A Sourcebook.* New York: Paulist Press, 1972.

Johnson, D. W. *Learning Together and Alone.* Englewood Cliffs, NJ: Prentice-Hall, 1975.

Joyce, B. R., & Weil, M. *Models of Teaching.* Englewood Cliffs, NJ: Prentice-Hall, 1972.

Lippitt, R., Fox, R., & Schaible, L. *The Teacher's Role in Social Science Investigation.* Chicago: Science Research Associates, 1969.

Miel, A. *Cooperative Procedures in Learning.* Westport, CT: Greenwood Press, 1972.

Olmstead, J. A. *Small Group Instruction: Theory and Practice.* Alexandria, VA: Human Resources Research Organization, 1974.

Stanford, G. *Developing Effective Classroom Groups: A Practical Guide for Teachers.* New York: Hart Publishing Co., 1977.

Thelen, H. A. *Education and the Human Quest.* New York: Harper and Row, 1960.

Zinberg, N. E. *Teaching Social Change: A Group Approach.* Baltimore: Johns Hopkins University Press, 1976.

8
The Role-Playing Model

Role playing provides pupils with practice in acting out situations. This can make them more aware of their own values and opinions and help them better understand how people affect one another's behavior. This model[1] is based on the assumption that, in the process of enacting a variety of roles, children will learn concepts about human behavior that can be generalized into real-life situations.

Introduction

PART 1. A Classroom Example

PART 2. Procedures for Using the Role-Playing Model in the Classroom

PART 3. Settings Needed When Using the Role-Playing Model

PART 4. Anticipated Student Outcomes of Using the Role-Playing Model

PART 5. Checklists for Evaluating a Program Based on the Role-Playing Model

PART 6. References and Resources

Introduction

Role playing demands that pupils temporarily step out of their usual behavior patterns and try on the behaviors, background, and feelings

of other people. This playing out of roles should take place in a circumscribed and nonthreatening atmosphere. During role playing, pupils
can engage in interpersonal problem solving and improve their understanding of why people do what they do. The insights they gain by
partaking of this type of activity can often be transferred to real life.

The first role-playing teaching model was developed by Fannie and
George Shaftel,[2] who worked for twenty years at teaching children to
practice such democratic ideals as integrity, justice, and compassion in
everyday life situations. Although techniques similar to role playing can
also be found in psychodrama (a therapy technique which should be used
only by trained clinicians), role playing as presented here differs from this
technique in intent and method. Used in the classroom, role playing is a
method for social learning rather than for obtaining deep insights into
oneself.

Basically, the role-playing model calls for a group of pupils to discuss a
situation, propose and enact the characters' next steps, evaluate these
steps and their consequences, and then propose a solution or solutions to
the problem situation. Through this process, pupils may come to understand the consequences of their own choices in real life, as well as to
realize that outcomes are often determined not only by their own actions
but also by the opinions and behaviors of others over whom they have no
control. The role-playing experience can help children develop skill in
areas such as observation, influence, empathy, and decision making. It
has been found to be especially useful in the teaching of social studies
and literature.

Assumptions of the role-playing model

1. Pupils can learn to define, confront, and cope with many commonplace interpersonal problems.
2. Pupils can learn to become aware of the values, impulses, fears,
   and external pressures that tend to influence their own and others'
   actions.
3. Pupils can apply to real situations the insights they have gained in
   role-playing situations.
4. Pupils can test their own ideas, opinions, and behaviors through
   simulated interactions.
5. The "trying on" of roles can lead to an in-depth understanding of
   problems and situations.
6. Learning how to play roles can improve pupils' interpersonal skills
   and increase their awareness of their own motives and those of
   others.

Part 1: A Classroom Example

While preparing a unit on the early frontiersmen for his fifth-grade pupils, Mr. Kane thought that his children would gain an empathetic understanding of the life of the early Americans through role-playing activities. He hoped that they would see that the problems faced by the families who crossed the plains in covered wagons were similar in certain ways to the problems facing families today.

Select the role-playing situation.

To prepare his students, Mr. Kane first had them read about the life of the early American settlers. He also took them to see a special museum exhibit on the housing, tools, and transportation used by the settlers. Then he chose simple situations (making tools and building shelter) that lent themselves to role-playing activity.

Prepare for role playing.

The class had difficulty at first. Some pupils became self-conscious and acted silly. For example, while one group "acted out" the problems of building a raft as a means of getting a wagon across the river, the rest of the class made teasing comments. There was also a lot of giggling and squirming.

Mr. Kane stopped the enactment and discussed with the class the purposes of role playing. Everyone agreed that it was a good thing to do, but said that it made for nervousness and embarrassment. Mr. Kane emphasized that the ideas were what were important, *not* the acting ability of the pupils.

Mr. Kane then decided to have the class practice acting in smaller groups. After everyone had the chance to experience what it was like to act "as if" he or she were someone else, he reintroduced the idea of role playing to the entire class. "Remember the problem we discussed about two settlers wanting the same piece of land?" he asked. "What were the two families to do? We found that sometimes it isn't easy to decide what to do when a great deal rides on the decision.

"Today I'm going to read 'Carrie's Burden,' a story about a girl who had a problem that grew worse after her family moved west. She felt that her family was treating her unjustly—that she was being punished for something someone else had done."

"Oh, Mr. Kane," Jimmy called out, "can't you give us a story with a happy ending this time?"

"Happy and sad aren't always the best words to describe the various ways a problem can be solved. Let's take Carrie's story and think of how the words 'happy' and 'sad' apply. As I read this story, think of what *you* might do if you were in Carrie's place." (The story is summarized below.)

Carrie's family, who had lived for many years in a comfortable village, was moving west. Carrie was unhappy about leaving her friends, her teachers, her books. But Carrie's older brother Alan was thrilled with the adventures he was having. On the other hand, Carrie's younger sister Ellen cried herself to sleep each night because she was afraid of bears and Indians. She complained about not being able to wear good clothes, about her hard bed, and about the rough ride. And when there were chores to be done—and there were many—Ellen sulked and sniffled and complained until her mother finally said, "Carrie, you do it."

And Carrie would nod and do the job. Her older brother was usually too busy to help out, so Carrie would work from sunup to sundown, with little time left to her for reading or writing to her friends back home.

One day, a peddler came by. Carrie was thrilled with the wonderful things he carried with him: dolls, fabrics, tools, candies . . . and books. Oh, how Carrie would have loved to have a book!

Carrie's father told the children that each of them could choose something that cost fifteen cents. Alan chose a packet of rifle powder and a bag of candy; Carrie chose a book; and Ellen chose a doll—a doll that cost thirty cents!

Father looked at Ellen and said, "Ellen, that's too expensive. You must choose something that costs less." But Ellen only screamed and cried. She threw herself on the ground. She threw the doll down, too. It broke and its face was all scratched. Mother took Carrie aside. "Carrie," she said, "we will have to pay for the doll. I'm afraid you will have to give up the book. Next time we will get you something. Ellen's still young—she is only seven, and she's been so unhappy since we moved." Carrie said, ". . ."

After reading the story, Mr. Kane waited for a few moments for the class to think about it. Then he asked, "What do you think Carrie should say to her parents?"

"I think it's about time Carrie gets something," Margaret said. "I think she should tell her father it was Ellen's fault—that she shouldn't have to pay for Ellen's mistake!"

"But what can Carrie do?" asked Bill. "The doll is ruined. Somebody has to pay for it!"

Select the participants.

At this point Mr. Kane felt it was important to give Margaret a chance to work out her ideas. "Would you come up here and play Carrie, Margaret?" Mr. Kane asked. "Bill can play the father. Who would like to play the mother?"

Several children raised their hands.

"All right, Jo. Why don't you come up here?"

"We should also have someone play Alan," Bill suggested.

Ed volunteered for this role. Mr. Kane quickly moved a table to be used as the peddler's wagon. "What part are you going to start with, Margaret?" he asked.

"Maybe the mother should start," Jo said. "I could begin by asking Carrie to give up her book."

"Fine," Mr. Kane said. He turned to the class. "Now the rest of you watch and decide whether Margaret's way of ending the story could really happen. OK, Jo. Begin."

MOTHER: Oh, this is terrible. The doll's broken. And poor Ellen. She's been so unhappy. And now this. What will we do? We have to pay for the doll. Carrie, I know it's hard for you to do, but you must give up your book. We'll get you another one next time.

CARRIE: But, mother, that's not fair! I haven't had a book in such a long time! Ellen always gets what she wants. I'm going to ask Father for the money!

(Carrie goes to her father.) Father! Father! It's not fair that I have to give up my book. Ellen is the one who ruined the doll. How come I'm getting punished? The peddler may not come back for months!

FATHER: I know, Carrie. But you're older. If I had the money, I would gladly give it to you for your book. It hurts me more than it hurts you. But that's the way life is, and I don't want to hear any more about it.

(At this point Margaret seems stuck and doesn't say anything.)

"Well, what do you think of the idea so far?" Mr. Kane asked the class after several moments of silence.

"My mom always says, 'It hurts me more than it hurts you.' Then she punishes me," Bob said.

"Well, what can the father do? If he doesn't have the money, he just doesn't have it!" one of the other students, named Terry, commented.

"Wait, let's take the scene a little further," said Ed, who was playing Alan. "I have something to say."

(The enactment continues.)

ALAN: Mom, Dad, I won't get anything. Let Carrie have her book. I'm a boy; and I'm going to make things OK for Carrie. I'll wait until next time.

CARRIE: No, Alan. I can't let you do that. Your gunpowder is more important than my book. I'll wait until next time.

"All right," said Mr. Kane, interrupting. "Let's stop and talk about this resolution to the problem. Do you think it could have happened this way?"

Discuss and evaluate the enactment.

The discussion which followed reflected the children's differing attitudes toward the need to "indulge" a younger child at the expense of an older child. They also discussed the question of whether boys and girls were expected to do things differently from one another in the olden days. There was general consensus that the situation might indeed have gone the way it did, though some of the pupils were not happy with that solution.

"Why is gunpowder so important?" asked Heather. "I think the mother and father should flip a coin between Carrie and Alan and then do something special for the kid who loses—like giving time off from chores or something."

"I think they should send Ellen back to where she used to live and let her stay with relatives," said Jackie.

"Hold it, hold it, one idea at a time," Mr. Kane laughed. He thought for a moment. "Jackie had an idea—she said that perhaps Ellen should go back to her old village and stay with relatives. How might that idea work out? Heather, we'll get back to your idea later. OK?"

"If they sent Ellen back, everyone would be happy," Jackie said.

"How is she going to get back there?" Tom asked.

"They could ask the peddler to take her, or they could find someone else," Bryan said.

"But Ellen's too young to make the trip!"

"Maybe she doesn't even want to go," Bryan said.

Mr. Kane then set up the second enactment, with Jackie (playing Carrie) asking Bryan (the peddler) how Ellen might be returned to her village. The "parents" stood nearby, listening. Mr. Kane also asked one group of observers to pay close attention to how the people in the enactment were feeling, and still another group to judge how practical the members thought the solution was.

The second enactment, a discussion, and even further enactments then followed.

Part 2: Procedures for Using the Role-Playing Model in the Classroom[3]

In the pages that follow, you will find listed and discussed six steps for using role playing in the classroom. (See Figure 34.) Although they are

Figure 34. Steps in Using Role Playing

---

1. Select the role-playing situation.

2. Prepare for role playing.

3. Select the participants.

4. Prepare the audience.

5. Enact the roles.

6. Discuss and evaluate the enactment.

---

presented in sequence, you may not always use them in this particular order. You may even find that you have to repeat or review certain steps with your pupils. The amount of time you will need for any one step will vary, depending upon the interests and abilities of your pupils.

1. Select the role-playing situation.

Role-playing situations can be developed from several sources—from interpersonal problems arising in the classroom, from current issues reported in the newspapers, from literary and historical situations, etc. At first, you may want to choose the role-playing situations; later on, your pupils should suggest them.

Three general principles govern the selection of role-playing situations:[4]

1. *The situation or problem should have several possible interpretations, solutions, or endings.* Whatever "topic" you choose, it should be one that children can act out in different ways, depending on their experiences and points of view. Situations that involve a choice between what at first appear to be equally unsatisfactory alternatives are usually interesting and effective ones.

Here is a situation that meets this criterion. Sally tells her friend Ann that she has heard Jane telling everyone that Ann stole something. What should Ann do?

There are many possible courses of action; for example:

• Ann could do nothing.
• She could talk to Jane.
• She could get Sally to talk to Jane.

2. *The situation or problem should not threaten anyone's right to privacy.* Episodes that are too personal and that could relate to someone in the

class should obviously be avoided. However, classes that have developed an open atmosphere where pupils have had practice in freely discussing values, insights, and feelings are usually able to handle more sensitive, controversial situations than those in which role playing is a new experience.

When dealing with interpersonal, rather than with subject-related situations, try to present situations which are similar to those confronting your children. As the class gains in understanding, role-playing activities can come closer to real-life situations. For example, "The Sneetches" by Dr. Seuss[5] could be used as a vehicle for exploring feelings about discrimination based on someone's appearance. The story line runs as follows:

> The star-bellied Sneetches feel that they are better than the Sneetches without stars, so they do not invite the plain-bellied Sneetches to their parties, games, etc. A Fix-It-Up Chappie, Sylvester McMonkey McBean, then offers to put stars on the plain-bellied Sneetches for a small fee. And the plain-bellied Sneetches are made into star-bellied Sneetches. The new star-bellied Sneetches then march up to those who snubbed them. . . . (Role playing could start from here.)

3. *Some aspect of the situation or problem should be familiar to the pupils; they should be able to draw on their own experience while role playing it.* Pupils should be able to imagine themselves actually implementing the solutions, and really coping with the situation. They should also be able to relate to the feelings of other people, even if they have to do some research on the new situation. For example, the role-playing situation that follows is one which would interest children but for which they probably would not have the necessary background to know what options exist (or existed) for a doctor with impaired vision. Therefore, the class would have to prepare for such an enactment by doing some concrete research on this subject.

Elizabeth Blackwell, The First Woman Doctor

Elizabeth Blackwell had a very difficult time getting into medical school. Medical schools had never heard before a woman wanting to become a doctor!

She was finally admitted to a medical school, but only because the students wanted to play a joke on their teachers and so voted that she be accepted into the school.

In 1849, Elizabeth graduated. She went to visit the largest maternity hospital in France. Though she was not allowed to be called "Doctor" there, she was allowed to work in the wards and operating room as an aide.

One day while she was tending a baby with an eye infection, some of the infected material got into Elizabeth's own eyes. She became ill and lost the sight of one eye.

Elizabeth knew that a doctor with impaired sight could not perform certain functions, such as surgery. What could she do? (Role playing could start from this point in the story.)

2. Prepare for role playing.

When role playing, children commonly respond in terms of what they think the teacher expects of them, rather than express their own feelings and reactions. Use every opportunity, therefore, to convince them that they run no risk by expressing their honest feelings—indeed, it is just such feelings you are after.

1. *Introduce the situation.* For your pupils to "get into" a particular situation, they must first become involved and interested in the problem story, photograph, or narrative. They should also understand just what is happening in the situation that is to be role-played. Ask them to remember when they felt angry or sad, and so on. Ask them to tell you about something that happened to them that is similar to what happened in the role-playing situation. Or relate the problem to a recent class experience; for example: "Although this story happened a long time ago, something like this happened in class yesterday. Can you remember what it was?"

In addition to involving the children emotionally, make sure that the children have a "feel" for the circumstances surrounding the action that is about to take place. If necessary, they should read about or discuss the problem in order to understand the setting, characters, and emotions. In short, they should create an "image" of the people in the story and the circumstances surrounding the situation.

2. *Set the stage.* Setting the stage provides the class with a smooth transition from the introduction to the actual role playing. If the situation is an historical one or one taken from a literary scene, the children may need considerable help "getting into" their roles. In this case, provide them with background information, for example, what daily life was like for the people they will be portraying.

The pupils should also do some planning beforehand. You might invite them to plan a scene by asking, "Who will you need to help you portray your idea?" or "What might you want him to do?" No actual dialogue should be prepared, however, since role playing is most effective when the players have a chance to react spontaneously to one another.

After the general line of action has been delineated (but before the scene begins), you can help the players clarify their ideas by asking such questions as "How are you feeling at this point?" and "What have you been doing prior to the scene?" It often helps to arrange the furniture or to raise questions about the imaginary setting: "Where is this taking place?" "What's it like in this place?" "Is this taking place after school?" "Can you show us the windowsill where the money has been left?"

If the children need a prop, draw a picture on the chalkboard, place a chair in a position to represent a particular piece of furniture, or delineate areas where the scene will take place. Don't get elaborate, though. Remember, simple props are the most helpful.

3. Select the participants.

After the children warm up and start offering ideas, invite individuals to act out their ideas on how to end the story. ("Let's try out your idea, Jan, and see what happens.") Some friendly persuasion may also be needed at first. Rather than assigning roles, invite pupils to participate. ("How about it, Joe? Do you think you would like to take on the role of the ranch hand?")

When selecting role players, choose those children who have demonstrated by their comments that they have identified with the characters and so have an "image" of the roles they are to play. For the first enactment, avoid choosing (if possible) a child who is likely to offer an overly adult-oriented, socially acceptable solution. Having such a solution presented at the start of the role-playing activity may serve as a damper on what many children think and feel in similar situations. Children learn more by exploring for themselves the consequences of socially unacceptable solutions than they do by being obliged to act out socially accepted responses.

Sometimes you may select a child to play a role in a certain manner—a "strict" father, a "teasing" younger brother—because such attitudes are commonplace in many of the pupils' lives. At other times, you may select a child to play a part because you believe it will be useful for him or her to "try on" another role—the "popular" child playing the part of the "new child" in school who knows no one. But, whatever you do, don't push a reluctant child into role playing. A little encouragement may help such a child decide to participate, but ultimately he or she must make this choice.

4. Prepare the audience.

The roles have now been assigned; the enactment is about to begin. Before it does, however, prepare the rest of the class to be active, intelligent observers. Your objective, after all, is that both the audience and the role players learn from the enactment.

If your audience is not prepared, it may be hypercritical, inattentive, or so consumed by its own thoughts that it will not hear or see anything of what is going on. Or certain individuals may be too busy waiting for their own turn. Teach the children to be good observers—attentive, courteous, responsive, and alert. A true observer does three things: First, he or she remembers and describes accurately what was seen and heard; second, he or she interprets what was seen and heard; third, he or she reviews and evelutes the performance according to some established criteria.

Children can develop such observational skills by being assigned specific tasks. ("Watch carefully—so you can tell us exactly what happened during the first minute of enactment." Or, "Pay special attention to what Mary says to her father.") After they become more experienced with role playing, assign them tasks demanding a more complex interpretation. ("As you watch the enactment, see if you can describe what kind of person Jim is. What does he say that tells you that? How does he act? What does he do with his hands? What about the expression on his face?" Or, "Pay special attention to how the people in the enactment express their feelings. Then, when the enactment is over, be prepared to tell the role players how you thought they were feeling. What did they do to make you think that?" Or, "During the enactment, watch one of the actors. Think about whether you would behave that way." Or, finally, "Watch the actors portray this idea. Do you think it could happen this way in real life?")

At first, everyone might be assigned to observe the same thing. After several role-playing sessions, you may wish to divide the class into groups and assign each group a particular observational task.

5. Enact the roles.

In enacting their roles, the pupils should try to "live" the situation by reacting spontaneously to one another and behaving in the same way they feel the people in the actual situation would behave.

Role playing can be done directly (the pupils act out the roles themselves) or indirectly (by the use of puppets and masks). The latter method is particularly indicated if the pupils are inexperienced, self-conscious, or shy. Props can also be used if the enactment involves behaviors that may be embarrassing to a child. In any case, it is important for the class to understand that the manner in which the actors portray their roles does not necessarily represent their own feelings; rather, they are simply "acting out" a role.

As your students get involved in their role playing, you can help them in several ways:

1. *Spontaneity.* The role players should continually be encouraged to behave naturally. Spontaneous expression is most likely to occur in an atmosphere where they feel safe, and where they receive appropriate emotional support from their peers and teacher.

2. *Focus.* Both performers and the audience should focus their attention on the idea being presented, *not* on the dramatic quality of the performance. Since the objective of role playing is for pupils to learn to think of alternatives and to develop an awareness of the probable consequences of behavior, the quality of the acting is not what should be ultimately evaluated. The role players should be made to realize that a "smooth" performance is not expected and that slips or awkward moments are acceptable. In short, the emphasis should be placed on whether the class feels that the portrayal is "true to life" or not.

An enactment can reveal not only what might happen in a particular situation, but also what could happen afterwards. To lead the class in this direction, ask questions like, "What happens next?" Or, "Let's see what's going to take place now."

3. *Troubleshooting.* Role-playing activities, like any other classroom activity, cannot be expected to go smoothly always. Here are some tips that may help to keep problems to a minimum:[6]

• If there is excessive laughter that grows out of nervousness or embarrassment, acknowledge the fact, discuss it briefly, and then refocus student attention on the enactment itself and the goal of that enactment.
• If the children are interrupting one another too much and not allowing one individual to have the chance to present his or her views, ask them to wait; they will have their own turn at some later point.
• If a role player forgets his or her role or becomes uncertain about time and place, stop the role playing for a moment and ask questions such as, "Who are you interacting with, John?" and "Does Father's response make you angry?"
• If you find that the pupils who are supposed to be observing are instead instructing the actors, remind them that it is time to "let Mary work out her idea" and that they will have a chance to work out their own ideas later.
• If the role players become silly, stop the role playing for a moment and ask them, "How would you *really* behave in this situation?" or "Are you showing what might *really* happen?" Also ask them questions that can help them get back into their roles. ("Jane, how do you feel about what Mother just said?")
• If, despite all your efforts, the enactment proves to be fragmentary or irrelevant, thank the role players, and then ask for other ideas.

• If the class becomes overexcited and noisy, terminate the session, and then discuss some of the reasons that can explain the unruly behavior. As part of this discussion, have everyone indicate what factors contribute to good role playing.

• If an impasse is reached and the actors need help, or if an actor is becoming too emotionally involved, encourage other actors to take over.

• If you see that the group is becoming bored or restless, cut the enactment short.

• If you feel there is any confusion about the details of the enactment or any ambivalence about the roles of the characters, have the players reenact the scene.

6. Discuss and evaluate the enactment.

Once the enactment has been completed, have the class use the insights it has gained in an ensuing discussion. Then have the situation reenacted. This discussion/reenactment cycle emphasizes the practice aspect of role playing. Through trial and error, and by exploring old ideas and trying out new ones, the class can be led to sound solutions.

Use your judgment in determining at what point to stop the cycle of discussion and reenactment. Clearly, there will be no reason to call a halt if your pupils maintain an interest in the situation, and if the enactments and discussions are productive and meaningful.

1. *Discussion and evaluation.* Research has shown that while "the actual taking of roles may have greatest influence on attitudinal change, it is in the give-and-take of discussion that problem-solving procedures are refined and learned."[7]

A discussion can help the role players to achieve the same vantage point as the observers. Since the observers are not as emotionally involved in the situation as the role players are, they tend to see more readily the consequences of proposed solutions, as well as alternative lines of action. Furthermore, discussion helps pupils learn from one another. The learning will be peer-reinforced rather than teacher-reinforced.

Try to guide the discussion so that the observers think along with the role players. To help them do this, have them focus on the action that has been presented by asking such questions as, "What happened?" and "How was Ivan feeling?" After an appropriate period of time, guide the discussion toward the consideration of alternative proposals. You can choose to reiterate some of the earlier comments that might lead to alternative actions. Or you can ask, "Is there some other way this problem can be solved?" "Can you think of another way the situation might end?" etc.

Remember, though, you do not want the children to evaluate the acting or the theatrical aspects of the enactment. Instead, the discussion should include an evaluation of the "idea" and whether or not the portrayal was "true to life."

2. *Reenactment.* During reenactment, new ideas should be tried, situations should be reinterpreted by new actors, and roles should be switched to give the pupils a chance to act out problems from a perspective with which they were previously in conflict.

These reenactments should not "unfold" haphazardly. You should lead the discussion, choose the actors, decide when to cut an enactment, and select which ideas you feel are the most fruitful.

After several enactments and discussions, help the children organize their thinking by summarizing the ideas that they have offered. Restate, or have them restate, their thoughts and feelings. Try also to bring them to a sense of closure about the ideas they have discussed and portrayed.

Part 3: Settings Needed When Using the Role-Playing Model

Materials

Your major task in using this model will be to find incidents and problems that are appropriate for role-playing activities in your classroom. Collect such potential material by observing your own pupils, by asking other teachers for stories, or by borrowing ideas from literature.

If a role-playing situation involves subject matter unfamiliar to your students, use pictures, show films, take them on field trips to museums, etc. In short, children should have or be presented with enough detailed information so they can clearly visualize how the people in the unfamiliar situation might behave, as well as the conditions and "realities" they might be facing.

You may even wish to start, together with other teachers, a joint file of ideas, stories, descriptive passages, and bibliographical data to be used for later reference.

Classroom organization

You should now be aware of the steps involved in using role playing in a classroom situation. However, different activities may call for different ways of organizing your class. For example, instead of involving all the students at the same time, you may choose to work alternately with them in small groups. If so, allow each group to gather the necessary background information for its own role-playing activity, and to discuss and propose solutions. All the groups could then take turns role playing in front of the class.

To give you a better sense of the variety of classroom organizations that can be used with this model, you will find below examples of how four different teachers approached this task.

Example 1. Ms. Jones thought that she could best establish a supporting and accepting climate for role playing by using small groups. From time to time, she would ask a few children to sit in a circle with her and to discuss some issue that had grown out of their reading. Once she felt that the children had learned to listen to one another and to accept each other's opinions, she tried to introduce some role-playing situation to half the class. However, this proved too distracting to the other children, who were supposed to be doing seat work. So she then tried to involve the entire class. Although a few children were disruptive at first, after a little practice the class was able to handle the role playing with few problems.

Example 2. Mr. Evans felt that his classroom had the right atmosphere for role playing. At first he introduced problem situations familiar to the children, which the entire class discussed. He next had the children role play different solutions and divided the observers into separate groups for various observer tasks. Then the entire class participated in the ensuing discussion and reenactments. The children seemed to have no problem changing back and forth from role players to observers.

Example 3. As a group, Mr. Barone's pupils had difficulty listening to one another. They all wanted to talk at once. So he showed them a film about active listening. Then he paired pupils and had each pair practice a number of listening exercises. After this, he had the pairs meet together and practice listening in small groups. Finally, role playing was tried in expanded groups, with each group periodically evaluating how successfully its members listened to one another.

Example 4. Ms. Kamiya wanted to use role playing as a way of sensitizing and broadening her children's understanding of historical events. So she had the children familiarize themselves with the historical context of the events they had been learning in class via field trips to museums, independent reading and research, small group work, etc. Once the children had accumulated sufficient knowledge to venture beyond the simple historical facts, they participated as a class in listening to a situation, setting up enactments for it, role playing the enactments, and then discussing and evaluating what they had achieved.

Personnel

Role playing is often used with only a single classroom teacher guiding the activities. If you wish to divide the class into small groups, however, or if you have a few pupils who tend to be disruptive, you might consider using a teacher's aide or some other helper (perhaps an older child) who can work with each of the groups or engage nonparticipating children in some other activity.

A word of caution here: All those whom you enlist to help you with the role playing should have an accepting, supportive attitude toward the children and their ideas. In other words, they must maintain the warm climate that you have established, and they must understand the objectives of role playing.

Schedule

Role-playing activities can be scheduled quite flexibly. For example, the discussions and reenactments may be stretched out over a period of time if the class needs to develop more sensitivity, if many ideas have been offered for exploration, or if the children need more leeway to explore possible alternatives and solutions.

The way you answer the following questions may well influence the schedule you choose to set up:

• Is the climate in the classroom conducive to a frank expression of ideas and to spontaneity? If not, what can be done to change the atmosphere?

• How long should it take me to establish the proper climate?

• How much background do the pupils have in the kind of role-playing situations I want to introduce?

• How long will it take them to acquire the necessary background? (If the role playing involves common problems/situations in the children's everyday lives, only a brief time should be necessary.)

• How will I know when they are ready to begin role playing?

• Should I introduce activities to sensitize them to the issues they will be exploring in the role-playing situation? If so, how much time should I allocate to this task?

• Are my children likely to solve the "problem" to their satisfaction with just one round of discussion or reenactment, or should I plan for several rounds?

Figure 35 is extracted from a teacher's lesson-plan book, which included a sample schedule for role-playing activities.

Figure 35. Sample Schedule

Six-Week Literature Unit Using Role Playing

THEME: WHAT IS A FRIEND?

Summary of Teacher Tasks

- Select and prepare role-playing situations.
- Prepare supplementary reading lists to be handed out to pupils; then assign readings.
- Prepare descriptions of writing assignments to follow up on reading assignments.
- Read pupils' papers and provide feedback.

Summary of Classroom Activities

- Small-group discussions about feelings engendered by friendships (good and bad feelings); small-group discussions about viewing a situation from the other person's perspective and possible advantages in doing so.
- Classroom discussions about problems with friendship identified in assigned reading; classroom discussions about the differing perspectives of fictional characters.
- Role-playing activities (warming up, setting the scene, etc.) and discussions of enactments.
- Writing assignments (homework) based upon reading assignments.
- Writing assignments (in class) evaluating the results of role playing and discussing the insights gained from this experience.
- Writing assignment (at beginning and end of unit): "What Is a Friend?"

Summary of Time Frame

Week 1 Introduction of unit; small-group discussions; warming up for role-playing activities; writing assignment: "What Is a Friend?"

Weeks 2–5 Reading and writing assignments; classroom discussions; role-playing enactments and discussions; films followed by discussions.

Week 6 Small-group role-playing activities, with each group organizing and carrying out its own enactment. Preparation by each group of evaluation of enactments. Repeat of written assignment: "What Is a Friend?" (based now on work of the past five weeks).

Part 4: Anticipated Student Outcomes of Using the Role-Playing Model

This section provides a list of skills that children may acquire from participating in a program based on the role-playing model. The list is by no means exhaustive, so add to it and/or adapt it to the specific needs of your pupils.

The student outcomes listed below are written at two levels of specificity. Program objectives appearing in the left-hand column are general; related behaviors will be found in the right-hand column.*

Program Objectives	*Related Student Behaviors*
The pupil will feel free to express his or her view to others, either orally or in writing, and will recognize the right of others to do the same.	1. Will listen to another opinion without interrupting and injecting his/her own view 2. Will make relevant comments about an opinion given by a classmate 3. Will express own view without having to first determine the majority view 4. Will express own view without having to first consult the teacher 5. Will express own feelings and opinions in the enactments, discussions, and written assignments.
The pupil will convey his or her idea(s)—through either action or speech—on how best to resolve an open-ended situation.	1. Will be able to react and respond to others as he or she feels the characters involved would react and respond 2. Will enact a scene without expressing concern about being frightened or feeling silly 3. Will enact a scene with little help from or consultation with the teacher 4. Will not ask the teacher or the class whether his or her idea is "all right" before he or she enacts a scene 5. Will talk about the consequences of a solution after it has been proposed.

*All outcomes should be rewritten in terms of your particular subject area.

Program Objectives	*Related Student Behaviors*
The pupil will discuss the ideas involved in a problem and the consequences of different solutions to it.	1. Will discuss the idea embodied in an enactment, rather than the quality of the dramatic portrayal 2. Will ask questions 3. Will be able to express agreement or disagreement with the proposed solution 4. Will be able to comment on whether or not a given solution would be feasible 5. Will be able to say how a particular solution might affect different people in the situation.
The pupil will envisage alternative courses of action in open-ended role-playing situations.	1. Will be willing to say how a particular character might resolve a problem situation 2. Will have more than one idea about how the situation might be resolved 3. Will provide explanations for alternative resolutions 4. Will identify solutions that suit one character more than another 5. Will suggest the consequences of various courses of action.
The pupil will enter into role-playing activities willingly and cooperatively.	1. Will respond and react to others as he/she feels the character involved would react and respond 2. Will enact a scene without exhibiting fear or shyness 3. Will role play with little help or consultation from the teacher 4. Will discuss the idea embodied in an enactment, as well as the reality of the dramatic portrayal 5. Will ask questions 6. Will watch a role-playing situation without interrupting the actors 7. Will volunteer to role play.
The pupil will describe, interpret, evaluate, and relate role playing to his/her own experiences.	1. Will describe the feelings of the different characters 2. Will guess why certain characters feel as they do

Program Objectives

Related Student Behaviors

3. Will relate the problems presented in the role-playing situation to his or her own problems and to those of others

4. After observing an enactment, will report accurately what took place

5. After observing an enactment, will explain the meaning of what was observed

6. Will be able to respond to only one aspect of a situation—for example, feelings—and report back on only that aspect

7. Will explain whether he or she thinks the enactment could actually happen

8. Will say whether or not his or her own actions would be similar to those that were role played.

Part 5: Checklists for Evaluating a Program Based on the Role-Playing Model

The following two sets of checklists can be useful in evaluating the effectiveness of your program. The first checklist indicates how closely classroom procedures reflect the role-playing model; the second checklist indicates whether or not your pupils are progressing according to your expectations.

Checklist 1

How closely do classroom procedures reflect the model?

	FREQUENTLY	SOMETIMES	SELDOM
• Role-playing situations are within the experience of the pupils.	☐	☐	☐
• Role-playing situations are open-ended, allowing for a variety of interpretations or conclusions.	☐	☐	☐
• Role-playing situations provide pupils with practice in making empathetic responses.	☐	☐	☐
• Role-playing situations provide pupils with practice in making predictions based on their own experiences.	☐	☐	☐

Checklist 1 (continued)

	FREQUENTLY	SOMETIMES	SELDOM
• Role-playing situations provide pupils with opportunities to interact spontaneously with one another in simulated situations.	☐	☐	☐
• Role-playing situations are sequenced so that there are preparations, enactments, discussions, reenactments.	☐	☐	☐
• All pupils are encouraged to volunteer their ideas and opinions.	☐	☐	☐
• All pupils are encouraged to respect the rights of others to express their ideas and opinions.	☐	☐	☐
• All pupils are encouraged to volunteer for role-playing assignments.	☐	☐	☐
• All pupils are encouraged to draw parallels between role-playing situations and their own experiences.	☐	☐	☐
• Teacher keeps the class focused on the ideas and opinions that are being presented rather than on the dramatic quality of an enactment.	☐	☐	☐
• Teacher makes enactment move smoothly by helping pupils resolve any problems that arise.	☐	☐	☐
• Discussions which follow enactments accurately reflect the ideas and feelings conveyed in the enactments.	☐	☐	☐
• Pupils are left with a sense of closure after a role-playing enactment is over.	☐	☐	☐
• Enactments stimulate new thoughts and ideas.	☐	☐	☐

Are pupils given practice in:

	FREQUENTLY	SOMETIMES	SELDOM
• Actively attending to the enactment?	☐	☐	☐
• Describing what has taken place in the enactment?	☐	☐	☐
• Articulating the ideas that emerge from an enactment?	☐	☐	☐
• Identifying differing points of view?	☐	☐	☐
• Presenting an argument for a given point of view?	☐	☐	☐
• Predicting the consequences of a given course of action?	☐	☐	☐
• Suggesting resolution(s) to an open-ended situation?	☐	☐	☐
• Enacting a variety of roles?	☐	☐	☐
• "Setting the stage" for an enactment?	☐	☐	☐

Checklist 2

Have pupils made progress in their ability and willingness to:

	YES	UNCERTAIN	NO		MOST STUDENTS	SOME STUDENTS	A FEW STUDENTS
• Volunteer freely their ideas and opinions?	☐	☐	☐	or	☐	☐	☐
• Listen to the comments of others without belittling them?	☐	☐	☐		☐	☐	☐
• Volunteer for role assignments?	☐	☐	☐		☐	☐	☐
• Volunteer to enact roles which call for the expression of ideas differing from their own?	☐	☐	☐		☐	☐	☐
• Refrain from commenting during the role-playing situation?	☐	☐	☐		☐	☐	☐
• Focus on the ideas rather than the dramatic quality of an enactment?	☐	☐	☐		☐	☐	☐
• Provide an appropriate setting for a role-playing enactment?	☐	☐	☐		☐	☐	☐
• Conduct an enactment smoothly?	☐	☐	☐		☐	☐	☐
• Describe with some accuracy the ideas and feelings conveyed in an enactment?	☐	☐	☐		☐	☐	☐
• Identify the different points of view within an enactment?	☐	☐	☐		☐	☐	☐
• Present an argument for a given point of view?	☐	☐	☐		☐	☐	☐
• Predict the likely and logical consequences of a given course of action?	☐	☐	☐		☐	☐	☐
• Suggest more than one resolution to an open-ended situation?	☐	☐	☐		☐	☐	☐
• Draw parallels between role-playing situations and their own experiences?	☐	☐	☐		☐	☐	☐

Part 6: References and Resources

Chester, M., & Fox, R. *Role-Playing Methods in the Classroom.* Chicago: Science Research Associates, 1966.

Joyce, B., & Weil, M. *Models of Teaching.* Englewood Cliffs, NJ: Prentice-Hall, 1972.

Joyce, B. R., Weil, M., & Wald, R. *Three Teaching Strategies for the Social Studies.* Chicago: Science Research Associates, 1974.

Lippitt, R., & Hubbell, A. "Role Playing for Personnel and Guidance Workers." *Group Psychotherapy,* 1956, *9,* 89–114.

Nichols, H., & Williams, L. *Learning about Role Playing for Children and Teachers.* Washington, DC: Association for Childhood Education International, 1960.

Shaftel, F. R., & Shaftel, G. *People in Action: Role Playing and Discussion Photographs for Elementary Social Studies.* Level A–D, California State Series. Sacramento, CA: California State Department of Education, 1971.

Shaftel, F. R., & Shaftel, G. *Role Playing for Social Values: Decision Making in the Social Studies.* Englewood Cliffs, NJ: Prentice-Hall, 1967.

APPENDIX
NOTES
GENERAL REFERENCES
INDEX

Appendix:
A Sample Program Plan

1. Identifying information

Program Name: Role Playing for Playground Peace

School: La Salle Elementary School

Principal: Ms. Antoinette Clay

Planning Team Members

Jonathan Ching	sixth-grade teacher
Maria Gonsalves	fifth- & sixth-grade teacher
Henry Stokes	fourth- & fifth-grade teacher
Mary Petrosko	third- & fourth-grade teacher
Ruth Roberts	parent

2. Summary of program plan

A number of incidents in the playgound in which older children provoked and teased younger children led a team of upper- and lower-grade teachers to plan a program involving role-playing activities which would improve the children's behavior. The program was scheduled to be taught in four classrooms and to be continued for ten weeks or longer at the discretion of the teachers. The evaluation of the program was intended to determine if the role-playing program actually reduced playground incidents.

3. Description of program and rationale for planning it

This new program is intended to improve playground behavior and reduce incidents of violence. The teachers at La Salle Elementary have become increasingly concerned over problems arising between the younger and older pupils in the playground. Several incidents were reported of older pupils "picking on" or teasing younger pupils. Parents of the younger pupils complained that their children came home crying and did not want to go back to school because the older children were intimidating them. In fact, one third grader had to be sent home during the school day because he had actually been assaulted by a group of older pupils.

A committee of upper- and lower-grade teachers and one parent decided to plan a program that would help older pupils learn how to empathize with and respect the rights of younger pupils. At the same time, the latter would be helped to express their feelings toward the older pupils. A decision was made to base the program on the role-playing model because it was felt that role playing would

- help pupils "air" their feelings
- make everyone aware that a problem existed
- help pupils consider the consequences of their actions
- provide them with the opportunity to examine their values and actions from alternative points of view.

4. Description of the instructional component

Program objectives and related student behaviors.

A. Pupils will feel comfortable expressing their feelings and opinions and will be able to listen to and acknowledge the feelings of others.
   1. Each pupil will listen to someone else talk, without interrupting or injecting his or her own view.
   2. The pupil will be able to accurately restate any opinion given by a classmate.
   3. The pupil will learn to make educated inferences about the opinions and feelings of people (fictional or real) based on what they say and do.
   4. The pupil will express his or own point of view, even when it differs from those of others.
   5. The pupil will express his or her feelings and opinions in enactments, discussions, and written assignments.
   6. The pupil will recognize that people can view a situation from a variety of perspectives.

B. Pupils will be able to participate in a role-playing situation.
   1. Each pupil will suggest props/actions that are relevant to a particular setting.
   2. The pupil will use information from his or her own experiences, or from materials he/she has studied to describe and act out a solution to a problem.
   3. The pupil will be able to describe how a particular scene might begin.

C. Pupils will be able to suggest and discuss alternative solutions to a problem in open-ended role-playing situations.
   1. Each pupil will be willing to make a guess as to how a person might resolve a problem in a particular situation.
   2. The pupil will suggest more than one resolution to this problem.
   3. The pupil will be able to provide possible reasons for alternate resolutions.
   4. The pupil will identify solutions to a situation that seem to suit one person better than another.
   5. The pupil will be able to guess at the probable consequences of a suggested course of action.
   6. The pupil will be able to describe how a given solution might affect different people in the situation.
   7. The pupil will be able to say whether or not he or she agrees with a given solution.

D. Pupils will then describe, interpret, evaluate, and relate role playing to their own experience in the playground.
   1. Each pupil will be able to speculate on why certain people feel as they do.
   2. The pupil will relate the problems presented in the role-playing situations to his or her own problems and those of others.
   3. After observing a situation, the pupil will be able to report accurately on what was said and what took place.
   4. After observing a situation, the pupil will explain the meaning of what was observed.
   5. The pupil will be able to say whether or not his or her actions would be similar to those being proposed.
   6. The pupil will be able to watch a single aspect of a situation and report on only that aspect.
   7. Given a number of conflict situations, the pupil will identify those individuals who enjoyed some gain at the expense of others.
   8. Given a number of conflict situations, the pupil will recognize a situation in which one party is unable or unwilling to fight back.

Activities. The program will be divided into the following units:

Unit	Purpose of Unit
1. Are you really listening to me?	• To encourage students to listen to one another without interrupting • To teach them how to restate what someone has just said as an indication that they have "heard" that person
2. Everyone has feelings.	• To encourage students to accept the fact that their feelings are legitimate and that everyone else has feelings too • To help them recognize and describe their own feelings without embarrassment
3. Not everyone feels the same way about something.	• To enable students to recognize and describe the feelings of people in stories or hypothetical situations • To get them to accept the fact that people can view a situation from a variety of perspectives, and that each of these can have merit
4. How can this particular problem be solved?	• To teach students how to role play and how this can lead them to explore alternative solutions to problems • To help them relate the role-playing activities to their own experience in the playground.

Sample activity guide

The name of this activity is *Paraphrasing*. It will help pupils achieve the following program objective: "Pupils will feel comfortable expressing their feelings and opinions, and be able to listen to and acknowledge the feelings of others." A related student behavior elicited by this activity would be: "The pupil will accurately restate an opinion given by a classmate."

Procedures

Teachers will	Pupils will
set up games, such as Telephone or Rumor Mill, which encourage	play these games, and thus increase their ability to restate

Teachers will	*Pupils will*
pupils to accurately restate the statements of others.	opinions, and to detect misstatements when these opinions are paraphrased.

Arrangements

Chairs in circle or chairs as usual
No special materials needed
No adults needed.

Comments

5. Administrative characteristics of the program

Pupils to be served

Four classes numbering 107 pupils:
    Sixth graders—32
    Fifth graders—30
    Fourth graders—28
    Third graders—17

Staff

Four teachers of the following classes:
    Sixth grade
    Fifth/sixth grades
    Fourth/fifth grades
    Third/fourth grades
Two teacher aides
One playground supervisor

Resources

a. Mimeograph machine, filmstrip projector, paper, pencils, bulletin board of large strip paper with felt pen, tape
b. Contemporary Drama Service. *Can of Squirms.* Downers Grove, IL: Arthur Meriweather, Inc., 1973.
c. Shaftel, F. R., & Shaftel, G. *People in Action: Role Playing and Discussion Photographs for Elementary Social Studies.* Level A–D, California State Series. Sacramento, CA: Department of Education, 1971.

d. Value series

People I Don't Know	These are study prints—i.e., photo-
My Friends	graphs with a teachers' guide on the
Respect for Property	reverse side. They were produced in
My School	1972 by Morris D. Westenberg, Jr.,
	BFA, Educational Media, 2211 Michi-
	gan Avenue, Santa Monica, CA 90404.

6. Description of the evaluation component

First phase. The first time the program is taught, the following evaluative questions will be posed:

- Which activities did teachers use? When and with what results?
- Has there been improved behavior in the playground after five weeks? After ten weeks?

Instruments used to collect this information will include:

- Teachers' daily records and a weekly diary/log.
- Teachers' oral questions to students about their reactions to each activity.
- Observation of playground behavior by trained observers at five- and ten-week intervals.

Second phase. After the program has been taught twice, the following evaluative questions will be posed:

- Has the program produced changes in the way students behave in the playground?
- Is it likely that these changes are the result of the program?

The design and instruments for collecting this information will be:

- A graph of the number and kinds of playground incidents involving the children over an eight-week period (kept by trained observers)
- Introduction of the program to several classes of students (without the knowledge of the observers)
- Examination of groups to indicate frequency and quality of the incidents, as well as to identify participants
- Blind interviews with program and nonprogram students to discuss their reactions to hypothetical playground conflict situations.

7. Description of the management component

Time Line

Tasks to Be Done	*Oct. Nov. Dec. Jan. Feb. Mar. Apr.*	*Personnel*
1. Order materials and text.	├──┤	1. Ching
2. Schedule class time.	├───┤	2. Gonsalves
3. Train teachers in program.	├───┤	3. Stokes, Petrosko
4. Develop specifications for teacher record-keeping and logs.	├───┤	4. Stokes
5. Train playground observers.	├──┤	5. Petrosko
6. Begin program in four classes.	├─────┤	6. Ching, Gonsalves, Stokes, Petrosko
7. Collect, analyze, and report back on teacher records.	├─────┤	7. Stokes
8. Collect playground observations.	├─────┤	8. Petrosko
9. Write a report on first round of program, and evaluate the program.	├──┤	9. Gonsalves

Notes

Chapter 1: Perspectives and Definitions

1. M. Weil & B. Joyce, *Information Processing Models of Teaching* (Englewood Cliffs, NJ: Prentice-Hall, 1978), p. 8.

2. B. R. Joyce & M. Weil, *Models of Teaching* (Englewood Cliffs, NJ: Prentice-Hall, 1972).

3. This book will contribute to your planning, especially if you use one of the five suggested teaching models. However, you will find something of use in this book even if you search elsewhere for a model, or abandon the model-based approach entirely. The sections on planning in groups, evaluating a program, and monitoring a program plan are generic to program planning and evaluation rather than particular to a teaching models strategy.

Chapter 3: A Planning Agenda

1. A measure of teacher attitudes toward children and how children learn, published by the Psychological Corporation in New York.

2. This model was developed from the findings of researchers in psychology and education who have investigated and documented how people, especially children, learn concepts. Among the researchers whose ideas were used in the development of this model are Jean Piaget, Hilda Taba, and Peter Martorella.

3. This model is based on ideas extracted from three programs on teaching creative thinking skills: M. Covington & R. Crutchfield, *The Productive Thinking Program* (Columbus, OH: Charles E. Merrill Publishing, 1972); E. DeBono, *Lateral Thinking: Creativity Step by Step* (New York: Harper and Row, 1970); and W. J. J.

Gordon, *The Metaphorical Way of Learning and Knowing* (Cambridge, MA: Porpoise Books, 1971). The conception of creativity is taken from the work of J. P. Guilford at the University of Southern California.

4. This model, constructed from components of developmental theory, was greatly influenced by the work of Jean Piaget. Although Piaget himself did not translate his theory into educational practice, others are currently attempting to do so.

5. This model was derived from two separate educational investigations, one carried out by H. Thelen of the University of Chicago, who is interested in the educational potential of group processes, and the other by R. Lippitt, R. Fox, and L. Schaible of the University of Michigan, who are interested in the educational potential of the social science research methodology.

6. This model, developed by Fannie and George Shaftel, is based on concepts of role theory developed in the field of social psychology.

7. Lynn Lyons Morris, (Ed.), *Program Evaluation Kit.* (Beverly Hills/London: Sage Publications, 1978.) Books in the kit include *Evaluator's Handbook; How to Deal with Goals and Objectives; How to Design a Program Evaluation; How to Measure Program Implementation; How to Measure Achievement; How to Measure Attitudes; How to Calculate Statistics;* and *How to Present an Evaluation Report.*

Chapter 4: The Concept Analysis Model

1. Although the ideas in this model were to some extent derived from the works of those whose names are cited in the text and notes, the overall conceptualization for the classroom application of the model is the work of the staff of the Center for the Study of Evaluation.

2. P. H. Martorella, *Concept Learning: Designs for Instruction* (Scranton, PA: Intext Educational Publishers, 1972).

3. J. Piaget, *Judgement and Reasoning in the Child* (London: Routledge and Kegan Paul, 1928). Used by permission.

4. Based on the Taba Social Studies Curriculum Project, which includes a number of texts and handbooks that were produced over a span of several years.

5. P. H. Martorella, *Concept Learning: Designs for Instruction* (Scranton, PA: Intext Educational Publishers, 1972), pp. 7–8. Copyright © 1972 by Harper & Row, Publishers, Inc. Reprinted by permission of the publisher.

6. Adapted from J. Bruner, J. Goodman, & G. Austin, *A Study of Thinking* (New York: John Wiley & Sons, 1956), pp. 41, 43. Copyright © 1956 by John Wiley & Sons. Reprinted by permission of John Wiley & Sons, Inc.

7. Some of the techniques used in this sample lesson are adapted from *Science Curriculum Improvement Study: Material Objects, Teacher's Guide* (Chicago: Rand McNally & Co., 1970). Used by permission.

8. Adapted from P. Tanabe & M. C. Durkin, *Teacher's Guide for People in States* (Menlo Park, CA: Addison-Wesley, 1973), p. T127. Used by permission.

9. See Martorella, *Concept Learning: Designs for Instruction.* This work devotes a chapter each to recent curriculum development in math, language arts, science, and social studies.

10. Paraphrased from Martorella, *Concept Learning: Designs for Instruction,* p. 180. Used by permission. See note 5. This concept analysis sequence is adapted from an approach called the Klausmeier-Frayer Scheme. See Frayer & Klausmeier in "General References."

11. This figure is adapted from one devised by Edith West in "Concepts, Generalizations, and Theories: Background Paper #3," unpublished paper, Project Social Studies, University of Minnesota, p. 8, no date. (Taken from Martorella, *Concept Learning: Designs for Instruction,* p. 46. Used by permission of the publisher and the author. See note 5.)

12. SCIS Science and Nuffield Math Materials, for example, provide concept-sequencing suggestions for teachers.

13. See Appendix on pages 95–97 for an explanation, based on Jean Piaget's theories, of the ways in which the thinking of children differs from the thinking of adults.

14. Adapted from Martorella, *Concept Learning: Designs for Instruction,* p. 39. Used by permission. See note 5.

15. Tanabe & Durkin, *Teacher's Guide for People in States,* p. T9.

16. Tanabe & Durkin, *Teacher's Guide for People in States,* p. T9. Used by permission.

17. Tanabe & Durkin, *Teacher's Guide for People in States,* p. T9. Used by permission.

18. Tanabe & Durkin, *Teacher's Guide for People in States,* p. T10.

19. Tanabe & Durkin, *Teacher's Guide for People in States,* p. T10. Used by permission.

20. Adapted from Tanabe & Durkin, *Teacher's Guide for People in States,* p. T37. Used by permission.

21. Some of these questions are adapted from C. Lavatelli, *Piaget's Theory Applied to an Early Childhood Curriculum* (Boston: American Science and Engineering, 1973), pp. 156–157. Used by permission.

22. Adapted from Tanabe & Durkin, *Teacher's Guide for People in States,* p. T37. Used by permission.

23. Piaget, *Judgement and Reasoning in the Child.*

24. Piaget, *Judgement and Reasoning in the Child,* p. 152. Used by permission.

25. Piaget, *Judgement and Reasoning in the Child,* p. 154. Used by permission.

26. Piaget, *Judgement and Reasoning in the Child,* p. 216. Used by permission.

27. Piaget, *Judgement and Reasoning in the Child,* p. 223. Used by permission.

28. Piaget, *Judgement and Reasoning in the Child,* p. 252. Used by permission.

Chapter 5: The Creative Thinking Model

1. Although the ideas in this model were to some extent derived from the works of those whose names are cited in the text and notes, the overall conceptualization for the classroom application of the model is the work of the staff of the Center for the Study of Evaluation.

2. J. P. Guilford & R. Hoepfner, *The Analysis of Intelligence* (New York: McGraw-Hill, 1971). The distinction between convergent and divergent thinking

originally appeared in J. P. Guilford, "Traits of Creativity," in H. H. Anderson (Ed.), *Creativity and Its Cultivation: Interdisciplinary Symposium on Creativity* (New York: Harper and Brothers, 1959), pp. 152–161.

3. Abridged and adapted from M. Covington & R. Crutchfield, *The Productive Thinking Program.* Used by permission.

4. Abridged and adapted from E. de Bono, *Lateral Thinking: Creativity Step by Step.* Copyright © 1970 by Edward de Bono. Reprinted by permission of Harper & Row, Publishers, Inc.

5. Abridged and adapted from W. J. J. Gordon, *The Metaphorical Way of Learning and Knowing.* Used by permission.

6. "Just suppose" is a term and technique used by Covington & Crutchfield in *The Productive Thinking Program.*

7. The technique of using analogies was adapted from Gordon, *The Metaphorical Way of Learning and Knowing.* Used by permission.

8. Ways of creating a climate fostering creativity were adapted from M. A. Wallach & N. Kogan, *Modes of Thinking in Young Children* (New York: Holt, Rinehart & Winston, 1965). Copyright © 1965 by Holt, Rinehart & Winston, Inc. Used by permission of Holt, Rinehart & Winston.

9. Techniques for developing creative ideas and products are only briefly described in this step. More detailed descriptions and examples can be found in the Appendix, pp. 120–131.

10. Most of the techniques presented in this model were adapted from three creative thinking programs mentioned earlier: Covington & Crutchfield, *The Productive Thinking Program:* de Bono, *Lateral Thinking: Creativity Step by Step;* and Gordon, *The Metaphorical Way of Learning and Knowing.* See the Appendix, pp. 120–131, for descriptions, examples, and citations for each technique.

11. "Role playing" is a method by which children interact with one another in spontaneous play-acting situations in order to explore their feelings and attitudes.

12. Techniques no. 10 and no. 11 use analogies to help stimulate creative thinking. "Making analogies" involves selecting two ideas or entities, and then exploring the connection or relationship between them.

13. De Bono, *Lateral Thinking: Creativity Step by Step.* Used by permission. See note 4.

14. Adapted from Covington & Crutchfield, *The Productive Thinking Program.* Used by permission.

15. Adapted from de Bono, *Lateral Thinking: Creativity Step by Step.* Used by permission. See note 4.

16. Adapted from Covington & Crutchfield, *The Productive Thinking Program.* Used by permission.

17. Adapted from de Bono, *Lateral Thinking: Creativity Step by Step.* Used by permission. See note 4.

18. Adapted from Covington & Crutchfield, *The Productive Thinking Program.* Used by permission.

19. Adapted from Covington & Crutchfield, *The Productive Thinking Program.* Used by permission.

20. Adapted from Covington & Crutchfield, *The Productive Thinking Program.* Used by permission.

21. Techniques no. 10 and no. 11 adapted from Gordon, *The Metaphorical Way of Learning and Knowing.* Used by permission.

22. Adapted from Gordon, *The Metaphorical Way of Learning and Knowing,* p. 26. Used by permission.

Chapter 6: The Experiential Learning Model

1. Although the ideas in this model were to some extent derived from the works of those whose names are cited in the text and notes, the overall conceptualization for the classroom application of the model is the work of the staff at the Center for the Study of Evaluation.

2. In G. E. Hein, "Piaget Materials and Open Education" (*EDC News,* Winter, 1973, *1*), the necessity for abolishing a work-play dichotomy is effectively argued.

3. In the same article cited just above, the author points out and explains the difficulty that "why" questions pose for children.

4. Edmund V. Sullivan, *Piaget and the School Curriculum: A Critical Appraisal* (Toronto: The Ontario Institute for Studies in Education, 1967), p. 29. Used by permission. It should be mentioned here that Dr. Sullivan does not endorse the ideas presented in this classroom example. In fact, he arrives at conclusions that even take issue with some of the assumptions in this model.)

5. C. Lavatelli, *Piaget's Theory Applied to an Early Childhood Curriculum* (Boston: American Science and Engineering, 1970), pp. 150–154. A list, its rationale, and instructions for its use are provided here. Used by permission.

6. Adapted from Lavatelli, *Piaget's Theory Applied to an Early Childhood Curriculum,* pp. 126–127. Used by permission.

7. For Lavatelli's specific objectives that relate to each of these categories, see Part 4 of this model: Anticipated Student Outcomes of Using the Experiential Learning Model.

8. Adapted from Nuffield Foundation, *The Duck Pond* (London: John Murray, Publishers; and New York: John Wiley and Sons, 1967). Used by permission of John Murray, Publishers.

9. Consult "General References" for existing curriculum materials based on Piaget's developmental theory.

10. M. L. Goldschmid & P. M. Bentler, *Concept Assessment Kit—Conservation* (San Diego: Educational and Industrial Testing Service, 1968), p. 4.

11. See Lavatelli, Nuffield Foundation, and Science Curriculum Improvement Study (in Part 6: References and Resources) for further information about instructional sequences and questioning techniques.

12. Adapted from Lavatelli, *Piaget's Theory Applied to an Early Childhood Curriculum.* Used by permission.

13. "When a child is able to conserve, he recognizes that certain properties, such as substance, weight, volume, or number remain unchanged in the face of certain transformations, such as changes in the object's form, color, or position"

(M. L. Goldschmid & P. M. Bentler, *Concept Assessment Kit—Conservation*. [San Diego: Educational and Industrial Testing Service, 1968], p. 4).

14. See note 13.

15. Adapted from *Science Curriculum Improvement Study, Material Objects: Teacher's Guide* (Boston: D.C. Heath and Company, 1967). Used by permission.

16. Sullivan, *Piaget and the School Curriculum: A Critical Appraisal*, p. 3. Used by permission.

17. Sullivan, *Piaget and the School Curriculum: A Critical Appraisal*, p. 3. Used by permission.

Chapter 7: The Group Inquiry Model

1. Although the ideas in the model were to some extent derived from the works of those whose names are cited in the text and notes, the overall conceptualization for the classroom application of the model is the work of the staff at the Center for the Study of Evaluation.

2. H. Thelen, *Education and the Human Quest* (New York: Harper and Row, 1960).

3. R. Lippitt, R. Fox, & L. Schaible, *The Teacher's Role in Social Science Investigation* (Chicago: Science Research Associates, 1969).

4. Thelen, *Education and the Human Quest*, pp. 81–82.

5. Figure 24 adapted from Lippitt et al., *The Teacher's Role in Social Science Investigation*, pp. 9, 84, and 85, and from Thelen, *Education and the Human Quest*, pp. 138–145. Both used by permission.

6. Some of the ideas in this section were adapted from Lippitt et al., *The Teacher's Role in Social Science Investigation*, pp. 9, 84, 85, and from Thelen, *Education and the Human Quest*, pp. 138–145. Both used by permission.

7. Adapted from Lippitt et al., *The Teacher's Role in Social Science Investigation*, p. 17. Used by permission.

8. Lippitt et al., *The Teacher's Role in Social Science Investigation*, p. 19. (Most of these question types and examples were taken directly from the source with only slight adaptations.) Used by permission.

9. Thelen, *Education and the Human Quest*, pp. 133–134. (Ideas in this section were adapted from among Thelen's criteria for effective working groups.) Used by permission.

10. If you would like more information about forming, working with, and maintaining inquiry groups, an excellent source of ideas and information is Lippitt et al., *The Teacher's Role in Social Science Investigation*.

11. Ideas about group difficulties were adapted from Lippitt et al., *The Teacher's Role in Social Science Investigation*, pp. 111–115. Used by permission.

12. Form for evaluation (no. 2) was adapted from Lippitt et al., *The Teacher's Role in Social Science Investigation*, pp. 117–118. Used by permission.

Chaper 8: The Role-Playing Model

1. Although the ideas in this model were to some extent derived from the works of those whose names are cited in the text and notes, the overall concep-

tualization for the classroom application of the model is the work of the staff of the Center for the Study of Evaluation.

2. See F. R. Shaftel & G. Shaftel, *Role Playing for Social Values: Decision Making in the Social Studies* (Englewood Cliffs, NJ: Prentice-Hall, 1967).

3. These steps were adapted from Shaftel & Shaftel, *Role Playing for Social Values: Decision Making in the Social Studies,* Chapter 5, pp. 64–84, especially pp. 64–65. Copyright © 1967. Used by permission of Prentice-Hall.

4. Ideas on the boundaries of role playing in the classroom were adapted from M. Chester & R. Fox, *Role Playing in the Classroom* (Chicago: Science Research Associates, 1966), pp. 16–17. Used by permission.

5. Summarized from Dr. Seuss, "The Sneetches" in *The Sneetches and Other Stories* (New York: Random House, 1961), pp. 3–25. Used by permission.

6. Suggestions for facilitating role playing were adapted from Shaftel & Shaftel, *Role Playing for Social Values: Decision Making in the Social Studies,* pp. 94–103. Used by permission. See note 2.

7. Shaftel & Shaftel, *Role Playing for Social Values: Decision Making in the Social Studies,* p. 79. Used by permission. See note 2.

General References

Alternatives and Decisions in Educational Planning. Fundamentals of Educational Planning No. 22. New York: Unipub, Inc., a Xerox Education Co., 1977.

Arends, R. I., & Arends, J. H. *System Change Strategies in Educational Settings.* New York: Human Sciences Press, 1977.

Bartel, C. R. *Instructional Analysis and Materials Development.* Chicago: American Technical Society, 1977.

Berman, L. M., & Roderick, J. A. *Curriculum: Teaching the What, How and Why of Living.* Columbus, OH: Charles E. Merrill Publishing Co., 1977.

Collins, B. E., & Guetzkow, H. *A Social Psychology of Group Processes for Decision-making.* New York: Wiley, 1964.

Craig, D. *Hip Pocket Guide to Planning and Evaluation: Manual and Trainers' Manual.* Austin, TX: Learning Concepts, 1977.

Douglas, T. *Group Work Practice.* New York: International University Press, 1976.

Doyle, M., & Straus, D. *How to Make Meetings Work: The New Interaction Method.* New York: Wyden Books, 1976.

Easley, J. A., Jr. "Seven Modeling Perspectives on Teaching and Learning—Some Interrelations and Cognitive Effects." *Instructional Science,* 1977, *6,* 319–367.

"Effects of the Use of Four Types of Teaching Models on Student Self-concept of Academic Ability and Attitude toward the Teacher." *American Educational Research Journal,* 1976, *13*(4), 285–291.

Fantini, M. D., Ed. *Alternative Education: A Source Book for Parents, Teachers, Students, and Administrators.* Garden City, NY: Doubleday, 1976.

Frayer, D. A., Fredrick, W. D., and Klausmeier, H. J., "A Schema for Testing the Level of Concept Mastery." Working Paper No. 16. Madison, WI: Wisconsin Research and Development Center for Cognitive Learning, 1967.

Gow, D. T. *Design and Development of Curricular Materials*. Pittsburgh, PA: University Center for International Studies, 1976.

Green, T., Ed. *Education Planning Perspective*. Atlantic Highlands, NJ: Humanities Press, 1977.

Harris, A. *Curriculum Innovation*. New York: Halstead Press, 1976.

Hill, W. F. *Learning thru Discussion*. Beverly Hills, CA: Sage Publications, 1969.

Hug, W. E. *Instructional Design and the Media Program*. Chicago: American Library Association, 1976.

Joyce, B. R., & Weil, M. *Models of Teaching*. Englewood Cliffs, NJ: Prentice-Hall, 1972.

Kohl, H. *On Teaching*. New York: Schocken Books, 1976.

McNeil, J. D. *Curriculum: A Comprehensive Introduction*. Boston, MA: Little Brown & Co., 1977.

Marbach, E. S. *A Creative Curriculum: Kindergarten through Grade 3*. Provo, UT: Brigham Young University Press, 1977.

Michael, D. L. *On Learning to Plan and Planning to Learn: The Social Psychology of Changing toward Future Responsive Societal Learning*. San Francisco: Jossey-Bass, 1973.

Miles, M. B. *Learning to Work in Groups: A Practical Guide for Members and Trainers*. New York: Teachers College Press, 1980.

Morris L. L. (Ed.). *Program Evaluation Kit*. Beverly Hills, CA: Sage Publications, 1978.

Phillips, G. M., et al. *Group Discussion: A Practical Guide to Participation and Leadership*. Boston: Houghton Mifflin, 1979.

Popham, W. J. *Educational Evaluation*. Englewood Cliffs, NJ: Prentice-Hall, 1975.

Schmuck, R. A., & Runkel, P. J. *Second Handbook of Organization Development in Schools*. Palo Alto: Mayfield Press, 1977.

Shaw, M. E. *Group Dynamics*. New York: McGraw-Hill, 1976.

Stallings, J. A. *Learning to Look: A Handbook on Classroom Observation and Teaching Models*. Belmont, CA: Wadsworth Publishing Co., 1977.

Stein, I. D. *Group Process and Productivity*. New York: Academic Press, 1972.

Weil, M., & Joyce, B. R. *Information Processing Models of Teaching*. Englewood Cliffs, NJ: Prentice-Hall, Inc., 1978.

Weil, M., & Joyce, B. R. *Personal Models of Teaching*. Englewood Cliffs, NJ: Prentice-Hall, 1978.

Weil, M., & Joyce, B. R. *Social Models of Teaching: Expanding Your Repertoire*. Englewood Cliffs, NJ: Prentice-Hall, 1978.

Zaltman, G., Florio, D. H., & Sikorski, L. A. *Dynamic Educational Change: Models, Strategies, Tactics, and Management*. New York: Free press, 1977.

Zander, A. *Groups at Work*. San Francisco: Jossey-Bass, 1977.

INDEX

233